Living with Hope

A Scientist Looks at
Advent, Christmas, and Epiphany

John Polkinghorne

Westminster John Knox Press
LOUISVILLE • LONDON

© 2003 John Polkinghorne

Published simultaneously in Great Britain in 2003 by the Society for Promoting Christian Knowledge.

First American edition
Published by Westminster John Knox Press
Louisville, Kentucky

PRINTED IN GREAT BRITAIN

04 05 06 07 08 09 10 11 12 — 10 9 8 7 6 5 4 3 2

Library of Congress Cataloging-in-Publication Data is on file at the Library of Congress, Washington, D.C.

ISBN 0-664-22749-X

Living with Hope

A Scientist Looks at
Advent, Christmas, and Epiphany

To the bishops,
clergy and people
of the Diocese of Ely

Contents

Preface

In many modern eucharistic liturgies the congregation is called upon to declare, 'Christ has died; Christ is risen; Christ will come again'. Christian belief requires a threefold perspective: towards the past, towards the present and towards the future. The first two of these perspectives receive a great deal of attention, as we think about the life of Jesus and the continuing life of the Church in the presence of its risen Lord. The third perspective is rather neglected in contemporary Christian thinking. I believe that this is because a lot of traditional imagery about ultimate destiny and the end of history has lost some of its power and credibility. When did you last hear a sermon about the second coming of Christ?

Yet coherent Christian faith, and confident Christian hope, require that we regain conviction in talking about what theologians call 'eschatology', the consideration of how God's saving purposes will find their final completion. An honest theology has to pursue this matter while facing the reality of human death – and even cosmic death, for the cosmologists assure us that the universe itself will eventually end in collapse or decay. Advent is a good time in which to begin such a task. These matters are not easy to think about, and inevitably there is some degree of speculation involved. This book is offered as a contribution to the Church's reflection on the ultimate purposes of God, in the hope that its daily, 'bite-sized' portions will prove digestible by those believers or enquirers who are concerned with the search for a credible hope of a destiny beyond death.

For the last 16 years I have had permission to officiate as a priest in the Diocese of Ely, and in gratitude for that privilege I dedicate this book to the bishops, clergy and people of that diocese.

I wish to express my gratitude to Simon Kingston of SPCK, who first suggested this project to me and who has taken an encouraging interest in its progress. Simon made a number of helpful suggestions about a draft of the manuscript, though I must, of course, acknowledge full responsibility for what is actually said.

I wish also to thank my wife, Ruth, for her help in correcting the proofs.

John Polkinghorne
Queens' College, Cambridge
Epiphany, 2003

Introduction

Advent recovered

The special Christmas catalogues from worthy charities start arriving towards the end of the summer. In October, the decorations begin going up in the streets. By November, the festive shopping spree is in full swing. Christmas makes itself felt long before 25 December. The churches are not immune to this frenzy of anticipatory activity. December is the month for carol services of all sorts. It is also the month of Advent. In many churches there will be an Advent wreath, with its four red candles successively lit on the four Sundays of that season, but it is the white candle in the middle, the one that will be lit on Christmas Day, that is the one on which most anticipation is likely to focus. It is carols, rather than the distinctive Advent hymns, that most of us want to sing. Poor old Advent! It has become a Cinderella season, mostly squeezed out of church life.

I think that this state of affairs is a great pity, for we need to recover the special spiritual resources of Advent. It is a penitential time in the Church's year, a season when priests wear purple, in contrast to the white that they will don at Christmas. If you think that penitential times are dominated by gloom and guilt, you may well be glad that Advent has come to be downplayed in this way. Isn't it just like religion to get all sombre and grim when everyone else is preparing for the jolly consumerist feast of Xmas? To think that way is actually to make a bad mistake. Penitential seasons are not about making us miserable, but instead they are concerned with helping us face reality. That is why the eclipse of Advent is a spiritual loss. We need to recover its resources just because we need to be able to take a steady look at the way things actually are. Advent gives us the opportunity to take seriously issues that most of the time we sweep out of sight at the back of our minds. It helps us to face up to reality. In Advent, we come face to face with themes like death, and the moral seriousness of life that is called judgement.

Advent also gives us the chance to think again about God and God's relationship with human beings in the light of two great facts of the Christian gospel: the fact that Christ has come and the fact that Christ will come again.

Advent preparation

Advent, of course, means a coming. It is a preparatory season in which we get ready to engage with two central aspects of the divine encounter with humanity. First, we are encouraged to make ourselves ready to recall yet again the first coming of Christ, to relive the historical story of the one who is born as a vulnerable and threatened baby, lives a wandering adult life and submits to a painful and shameful human death, all as acts of solidarity by God with the suffering of creation. Second, it bids us look ahead to the end of history, when the kingdom of God and the lordship of Christ, presently expressed in ways that are partially obscured from our sight, will ultimately be visibly vindicated and fulfilled.

A large part of our Advent preparation will be a careful consideration of how we ought to think about that difficult theme of the second coming. The New Testament speaks about it using vivid but perplexing images, such as the rending of the heavens and the sounding of the last trumpet. Our picture of the universe today is so very different from the triple-decker world (heaven–earth–hell) of the first century, that we have to ask ourselves what we can make of these images that seem so problematic to us. In this task we can be helped by having to think again about Christ's first coming.

Many Jews in the first century were looking for the coming of God's Messiah. Some of the pictures that they found in the Hebrew Bible, together with the natural longing of a subject people to be freed from the yoke of the occupying power, inclined them to think in terms of a kingly deliverer, a kind of powerful second David whose military success would give the Romans the come-uppance they deserved. All this was natural enough, but in fact Jesus proved to be totally different, which was one reason why many people found it so difficult to understand exactly who he was and what his role was to be in God's plans.

The strangest thing was that it turned out that the Messiah, when he came, was a *crucified* Messiah, not a military victor. To many of Jesus' contemporaries, this idea seemed nonsensical, a total contradiction in terms. With the benefit of hindsight, we can see how this unexpected kind of messiahship had been foreshadowed in Old Testament passages, such as the famous song of the suffering servant in Isaiah 53 ('He was despised and rejected by others; a man of sorrows and acquainted with infirmity … by his bruises we are healed'). Scripture was indeed fulfilled in Jesus, but in quite unanticipated ways that took most people completely by surprise. We have to be open to the possibility that the second coming will be as strange as the first coming, at least in terms of expectations based on an overliteral interpretation of symbolic images.

Advent hope

A word that intertwines with the themes of the first and second comings is 'hope': the hope that was proclaimed to the shepherds by the angels, of true peace on earth, together with the hope that there is a final destiny awaiting us beyond our deaths. Paul put together the three Christian virtues of faith, hope and love (1 Corinthians 13.13), but again there is a Cinderella effect at work, for people tend to neglect hope in favour of the other two. Not only is this a spiritual loss, but it also fails to recognize how deep-seated is the intuition of hope that lies within the human heart, despite all the strangeness and bitterness that we also see in the world around us.

Peter Berger, in a marvellous little book called *A Rumour of Angels*, encourages us to look for what he calls 'signals of transcendence'. By this he means ordinary everyday happenings which, if we stop to think about them for a minute, contain a kernel of something profound and significant. An example of such an incident would be the following: A child wakes up in the night frightened by a bad dream and a parent who goes to comfort the child says, 'It's all right.' Berger asks us to consider what is happening. Is the parent uttering a loving lie? For after all, a world with cancer and concentration camps in it looks very far from 'all right' in any straightforward sense. Yet Berger claims, and I agree with him, that the reassurance the parent utters is not a deception, but a true insight that is vital for the child to receive in its growing up into human maturity. In other words, there is a profound human conviction that ultimately all will be well, a belief that is a sign of the stirring of a deep hope within us. As part of our Advent exploration we shall have to seek to understand where this conviction of hope might find its basis. I believe that it arises from an almost unconscious perception of the steadfast faithfulness of God.

It is important to distinguish true hope from two other attitudes with which it is often confused: optimism and wishful thinking. The former springs from a calculation of how things may be expected to turn out, with the belief that in the end it will all prove not to be too bad. It is the feeling possessed by the person who thinks they know a 'certainty' for tomorrow's horse race. Wishful thinking, by contrast, is not at all concerned with probabilities, for it simply sails off into the blue of ungrounded longings. It is the feeling possessed by someone who daydreams how nice it would be if their modest weekly 'investment' in the National Lottery made them an instant multimillionaire. Neither of these attitudes is the same as hope, which neither tries to predict the future from the present nor neglects the constraints that the reality of the present imposes. Christian hope is open to the unexpected character of what lies ahead precisely because it relies on the faithfulness of a God who is always doing new things.

The Four Last Things

Much traditional Advent thinking centred on the Four Last Things: death, judgement, heaven, hell. Today, I suppose, they are the four last things that anyone would want to introduce into polite conversation. It is a commonplace to observe that death has become the great taboo subject of our society, a final event that must be hidden away from view and consciousness as much as possible. Yet this one great human certainty cannot so readily be suppressed, and in the privacy of their thoughts many people are only too aware of their mortality, even when death itself may be expected to lie some way in the future.

The Advent section of this book takes the Four Last Things week by week, considering the general theme on the Monday and looking at related Bible passages on the following Tuesday to Saturday. Sundays punctuate this rhythm, for they are devoted to somewhat different topics that are also connected with the Advent season. The book is designed to be used in any calendar year and so, due to the variable position of Christmas Day in the week, this inevitably means that in some years the readings connected with hell may be cut off by the arrival of the Feast. In the extreme case, when Advent 4 is also Christmas Eve (as in the case of the year 2006), then hell disappears altogether. Since I shall be arguing that hell is the place where acknowledgement of the reality of God has been deliberately excluded, there is a certain theological appropriateness in this infernal tendency to wane and disappear. I hope, nevertheless, that in such years readers will be able to find other days on which to consider the issues that the calendar has set aside. Indeed, I also hope that in any year readers might be able, if they wished, to detach the whole of this material from its calendrical setting and use it as a source for a sequence of meditative readings on serious themes, whatever the season.

Christmas

Eventually we reach the Feast of Christmas and, having properly prepared ourselves in the Advent fashion, we are surely entitled to celebrate the full 12 days of that joyful season. During this period, the readings centre on themes connected with the story of the birth and with the mystery of the incarnation. We are led up to the Feast of the Epiphany, traditionally associated with Christ's baptism as well as with his manifestation to the Gentiles. The new calendar allocates the baptism its own day on 7 January and the book closes at this point, the point at which the public ministry of Jesus began.

Advent 1

The end of the world

'But in those days, after that suffering, the sun will be darkened, and the moon will not give its light, and the stars will be falling from heaven, and the powers in the heavens will be shaken. Then they will see "the Son of Man coming in clouds" with great power and glory. Then he will send out the angels, and gather his elect from the four winds, from the ends of the earth to the ends of heaven.'

(Mark 13.24–27)

Powerful words, describing dramatic events. Many of the original readers may well have thought of them as predictions of what might literally happen in the near future, perhaps within their own lifetime. For us the images are striking, but tinged with an antique quaintness. The stars are not heavenly lamps that might tumble down from their celestial fixings, but they are indications of the vastness of the universe within which we live (100 billion stars in our galaxy alone, almost all of them too faint to be seen with the naked eye). Not too many contemporary Christians go around thinking that one day they might look up and see Jesus riding on the clouds like a Christianized Valkyrie. So is all this just baggage from the past, something that we would do best to jettison as fast as we can?

Not at all. It was *always* a mistake to take these images with a plodding literalism, but it would be an even greater mistake to throw away an understanding of the realities that they symbolize. This passage, taken from what is sometimes called 'Mark's little apocalypse' (as if it were a condensed

version of the much more extended, technicolour apocalypse of Revelation), presents us with two important
Christian truths: that this seemingly substantial world is not
going to last for ever, and yet the faithfulness of God and of
God's Christ will never come to an end. On this Sunday, the
beginning of Advent, it is the first of these thoughts on
which I want us to concentrate our attention: the theme of
eventual cosmic futility. The second thought, the everlasting
reliability of God, is one that will undergird all our thinking
in the course of this book.

Human recorded history is very short (a few thousand
years) in relation to the timespan of the universe (14 billion
years). That is why we are unaware most of the time that we
live in a world that is in a state of flux. Things change, but
they only change very slowly on a human timescale. It is also
a dangerous world, containing many threats to the continued existence of life. Sixty-five million years ago the
dinosaurs were knocked out by the disastrous effect of an
asteroid colliding with the earth. That gave the little furry
mammals, who were our ancestors, their evolutionary
chance. One day humanity might suffer a similar fate, if it
does not destroy itself earlier through its own follies such as
nuclear war. Even if our descendants do make it through all
these hazards, life on earth cannot go on for ever. One day
the sun will have burned up all its hydrogen fuel and it will
then turn into a swollen red giant, about the size of the
earth's orbit. No terrestrial life could possibly survive that
catastrophe.

But maybe by then life will have migrated elsewhere in the
galaxy. It is quite possible, but that would amount to no
more than a temporary reprieve. After almost unimaginably
long periods of time, the universe itself will also die, either
in the long drawn out dying whimper of a world that is continually expanding, while simultaneously cooling and decaying, or in the bang of a fiery collapse into the final big
crunch. Either way, freeze or fry, science tells us that there is
nowhere where life can succeed in going on for ever. There
will indeed be an End of the World.

Religion has to take these gloomy predictions with absolute seriousness. To do so raises the question of what God is actually up to in creation, if eventually it is all to end so miserably. The only answer – but a totally sufficient answer – is that science cannot tell us the whole story, for it does not know about the everlasting faithfulness of God. In that steadfast love of the creator for creatures lies the only possible ground for the hope of a destiny beyond death, either for ourselves, who are condemned to futility on a timescale of tens of years, or for the universe that is condemned to futility on a timescale of many tens of billions of years. We shall die, and the cosmos will die, but the final word does not lie with death but with God. As we shall be thinking in the course of this week, this does not mean that death is not real, but it does mean that it is not the ultimate reality. Only God is ultimate, and that is a sufficient basis to enable us to embrace the Advent hope.

Jesus dealt with this very point when he had his argument with the Sadducees (Mark 12.18–27). He reminded them that God is 'the God of Abraham, the God of Isaac and the God of Jacob' and he went on to say, 'The God not of the dead but of the living'. The reasoning is clear and convincing. If the patriarchs mattered to God once (and they did), then they must matter to God for ever. If you and I matter to God once (and we do), then we must matter to God for ever. And I think that we can also say the same about the whole created universe.

Prayer

> God is our refuge and strength,
>   a very present help in trouble;
> Therefore we shall not fear, though the earth change,
>   though the mountains shake in the heart of the sea.
> (Psalm 46.1–2)

Monday: Death

> *Then they went to a place called Gethsemane; and he said to his*
> *disciples, 'Sit here while I pray.' He took with him Peter and James*
> *and John, and began to be distressed and agitated. And he said*
> *to them, 'I am deeply grieved, even to death; remain here and keep*
> *awake.' And going a little farther, he threw himself on the ground*
> *and prayed that, if it were possible, the hour might pass from him.*
> *He said, 'Abba, Father, for you all things are possible; remove this*
> *cup from me; yet, not what I want, but what you want.'*
>
> (Mark 14.32–36)

Christian people sometimes talk about death as 'falling
asleep' or even, in words that are occasionally quoted at
funerals, as 'going into the next room'. I am not very happy
with this language. You can find the sleep metaphor used
occasionally in the New Testament (for example, in 1
Thessalonians 4.13 where, to disguise the fact, the transla-
tors of the NRSV have quite unjustifiably taken it upon
themselves to turn the original 'fallen asleep' into 'died').
But today's passage, which is one of the most moving and
holy in the whole gospel story, shows us with what seriousness Jesus himself faced his own approaching death. He is
'deeply grieved' – Luke (22.44) even speaks of 'sweat like
great drops of blood' – and he asks that if possible this cup
should pass from him. Yet he is also resolute to accept the
Father's will. Death is clearly in no sense a trivial or easy matter for Jesus.

People have often compared this scene with the end of
another famous figure in the ancient world, Socrates. He too
was unjustly condemned to die, in his case not by crucifixion
but by the much gentler process of drinking a cup of hem-
lock. Before he did so, he talked with his friends in a philosophical way about his belief in the immortality of the soul.
The discourse ended, Socrates then calmly took the poison
and tranquilly allowed it to bring about paralysis and eventual death. The contrast of this peaceful scene with
Gethsemane is very striking.

So what is happening? Is the Greek philosopher a nobler figure than the Jewish Messiah? To understand Gethsemane I think that we need to understand that the Christian hope is not belief in a spiritual survival, such as Socrates believed in, but it centres on the double process of death and resurrection. Even for Jesus the two are separated by the silent tomb of Holy Saturday.

I can best explain how I understand this by asking a related question. What should we believe is the nature of the human soul? Socrates thought that the soul was a purely spiritual entity which during this life was housed in the flesh of the body, but which would be released at death to enter into the immortal life of an unencumbered spiritual existence. Someone once caricatured this view as being the picture of a human being as a 'ghost in a machine'. It seems to me that today it is very hard for us to think in this Socratic way. What we know about the effects of brain damage on the mind, and of drugs on behaviour, suggest a much more unified, 'package deal' picture of a human being, understood as an integrated, animated entity. This idea would not have shocked or surprised the writers of the Bible, for it was also the way in which Hebrew people thought about being human.

But if that is the case, what has happened to the soul? Have we lost it? I don't think so. The soul is 'the real me'. Now what that could be is a bit of a problem even in this life, let alone beyond it. What makes me today the same person that I was 60 years ago? It is not, as you might think, physical continuity, for the atoms that make up our bodies are changing all the time, through wear and tear, eating and drinking. I have very few atoms that were in my body even three years ago, let alone 60. What really maintains the continuity of the real me is not matter itself, but the immensely complex, information-bearing *pattern* in which that matter is organized. That pattern is the soul.

It will be dissolved at my death with the decay of my body. Therefore, I have no *natural* expectation of surviving death. That is why death is a real end. Yet it is perfectly consistent to believe – and we can indeed believe – that the faithful

God will remember the pattern that was me, holding it in the divine memory, in order to reconstitute me again in God's great final act of resurrection, taking place beyond history.

I shall have more to say about this later. For the moment, just note that when God does bring about that re-embodiment, it will have to be in some new kind of matter, for if it were the old kind I would just have been made alive again in order to die again. And where will that new 'matter' come from? It will surely be the redeemed matter of this world, transformed by God after the death of the universe itself. The future of the cosmos and the future of humanity must lie together, in the life of that new creation that will succeed the demise of the old. Again, I shall have more to say about this later in relation to the resurrection of Christ, which is the pattern and the guarantee of the hope that we are given through the steadfast faithfulness of our creator.

Meanwhile, we can think of the moment of death as being the great final act of this life, in which we shall commit ourselves fully into the hands of God.

Prayer

> Still let me prove thy perfect will,
>   my acts of faith and love repeat;
> till death thine endless mercies seal,
>   and make the sacrifice complete.
>   (Charles Wesley)

Tuesday: The Fall – Mortality

Therefore, just as sin came into the world through one man, and death came through sin, and so death spread to all because all have sinned ... If, because of the one man's trespass, death exercised dominion through that one, much more surely will those who receive the abundance of grace and the free gift of righteousness exercise dominion in life through the one man, Jesus Christ.

(Romans 5.12, 17)

The story of Adam and Eve, the garden and the snake, is one
that still fascinates us. We do not at all have to take it literally
to feel its power. This is because it operates at the level which
– to use a dangerous word – is properly called 'myth'. That
word is dangerous because modern usage has debased the
meaning of myth to reduce it to amounting to no more than
a fairy story. But in Genesis 3 we are not encountering an
ancient tale on a par with the idea of the tooth fairy. Rather,
we meet with truth in so deep and powerful a form that it
can *only* be conveyed through a story. That is the true meaning of myth.

The Eden story is not about a disastrous ancestral act that
happened once upon a time, but it is concerned with what is
always true about the state of men and women. Its message
is that the root of the human predicament, manifested in so
much of the skewedness and shabbiness of life (the true
nature of sin is what a theologian would call it), is the belief
that we can go it alone, the feeling that we can do without
God. Thinking this way is the temptation that the serpent
whispers in Eve's ear, eat this and you 'will be like God', able
to please yourself, while all the time singing 'I did it my way'.
And that is a lie, for in fact we are creatures who depend for
our fullest good on a relationship with our loving creator. To
fall for the snake's trick is ultimately to opt for spiritual
death.

In these difficult verses from Romans, Paul refers back to
the story of Adam and Eve, linking together sin and death.
We know, of course, that physical death was around long
before there were any human beings. It was what did for the
dinosaurs and it is an indispensable part of an evolutionary
world, in which one generation has to make way for the
next. How then should we think today about the story of the
Fall? I tackle it this way.

I think that humans differ from even our closest cousins,
the higher primates, by being self-conscious. Of course, the
animals are consciously aware of the present and they can
look a little way ahead into the future (if the chimpanzee
throws the stick, maybe it will knock down the ripe banana).

We, however, can look very far into the future, even anticipating that one day we shall die, although that event may lie many years ahead. Some time in the development of our ancestors, this self-consciousness began to dawn. They then became fully aware of themselves as individuals, and also of the fact that death lay ahead of them somewhere in the future. I believe that at the same time our ancestors must have become aware in a new way of the presence of God. They therefore faced the pull of two centres of attraction, the individual self and God, and there began a process by which human beings chose to turn away from God and to curve into themselves. This rejection of the divine and concentration on the self was the Fall. It did not happen in a single instant, for it must surely have been a process of which we and all other human beings are now the heirs.

The Fall did not bring physical death into the world, but it did bring about the experience of what one might call 'mortality'. Our ancestors became aware of their future death, and at the same time they had become alienated from the One who is the only ground of the hope of a destiny beyond that death. The result was mortality, the feeling of sadness and bitterness at the inevitable transience of earthly lives. This was the way in which 'death came through sin'.

Christians believe that Jesus is both human and divine. He is the bridge that has been re-established between the life of the creator and the life of creatures, potentially abolishing the alienation of the Fall. I believe that this is what Paul is getting at in talking about Christ as a kind of second Adam who undoes the consequences of the first. What has been broken in the life of all human beings can be restored by Christ who, as Paul says in the preceding verse in Romans, is the one 'through whom we have now received reconciliation' (5.11). This is how it comes about that 'those who receive the abundance of grace and the free gift of righteousness exercise dominion in life through one man, Jesus Christ'. The Fall is a fact of human life and we see its effects all the time in the petty selfishnesses of daily life. Yet it is no more an ultimate fact than is death itself, for both can be overcome through the power and grace of God.

Prayer
Lord, draw us to yourself, that in life and in death we may know your gracious presence with us and so we may be delivered from faint-heartedness and fear.

Wednesday: The Pit – Little deaths

> *Save me, O God, for the waters have come up to my neck. I sink in deep mire, where there is no foothold; I have come into deep waters, and the flood sweeps over me.*
>
> (Psalm 69.1–2)

The ancient Hebrews seem not to have thought much about the possibility of life after death. They had a rather hazy notion of an abode called Sheol, where the shades of the dead were filed away, but it was a grey and dispiriting place, to say the least. The contrast with their neighbours, the Egyptians, with their intense preoccupation with providing for life beyond the grave, is very striking.

I think that one of the reasons for this strange gap in Hebrew thinking is that they were intensely concerned with the present life and with the way in which God is at work within the unfolding of this world's history. Hence the importance of the prophets in the Old Testament. Those prophets were often warning Israel of trouble ahead unless they changed their ways and looked more to God than to alliances with dubious neighbouring states. Yet trusting God in this life certainly did not imply an easy ride, free from all trouble, a lesson that the Jewish people had to learn with the greatest difficulty in the disastrous events of 587 BCE, which saw the Babylonian destruction of the temple and the carrying off of many of the leading people into a painful exile.

What was true in national life was also true for individual lives in Israel. Severe trouble could come on people even if they were seeking to live righteous lives. It is in the Psalms, with the great spiritual frankness that their writers display, that we find many pleas and protests to God arising out of profoundly difficult circumstances. An image that is often used by the psalmists is that of the Pit, as in the verses that we are considering today. It was a terrible place to be, stuck in deep mud and with the waters of chaos swirling around one. Yet the writers know to whom to turn in such extremity: 'Save me, O God, for the waters have come up to my neck'.

The image of the Pit is the symbol of the little deaths that come to all of us in life, on our way to that final death that will be the end of life on earth for us. In the New Testament, the corresponding image is the cross (the gallows instrument of painful execution) that we are called upon by Jesus to carry (Mark 8.34, etc.). These crosses are not to be sought in an excess of masochistic enthusiasm, but we are bidden to accept them as they come to us unsought. They take many forms: illness, acute or chronic; the opportunity that was denied us to use our talents to the full when we did not receive the promotion that seemed to be our due; disappointment that a relative or a close friend does not give us all the affection that we expect of them; the obligation to look after someone whose need for attention diminishes the room that we have for living our own lives. I could well go on for a long time without mentioning the particular cross that you have to bear, but we all have crucial experiences of this sort, of one kind or another.

God does not sweep away these problems by magic, for the preacher's cliché is true and we are not saved *from* trouble but *in* trouble. If we are able to accept these limitations that life brings, that will be the first step in our being able to transcend them. They are indeed little deaths that we must learn to die, and that learning can prepare us for that final death, in which all that will be left to us will be to commit ourselves into the hands of a faithful creator and merciful saviour. It is no bad thing for us to be aware of our mortality, for it is in this way that we can begin to come to terms with its reality. Another way in which we can prepare ourselves for our final day on earth is to pray regularly that we may be given the grace to make a good death when that time comes, so that indeed our last act will be one of trusting commitment to the steadfast love of God.

Prayer
God, our Father, we know that we must die. Grant that when that time comes for us, we may have your peace and be able to rest in the hope that you have given us through the resurrection of your Son, Jesus Christ, from the dead.

Thursday: Denial of death – The rich fool

> *Then he told them a parable: 'The land of a rich man produced abundantly. And he thought to himself, "What should I do, for I have no place to store my crops?" Then he said, "I will do this: I will pull down my barns and build larger ones, and there I will store all my grain and my goods. And I will say to my soul, 'Soul, you have ample goods laid up for many years; relax, eat, drink and be merry.'" But God said to him "You fool! This very night your life is being demanded of you. And the things you have prepared, whose will they be?"'*

(Luke 12.16–20)

Many of Jesus' parables linger hauntingly in the mind. The parable of the rich fool has that kind of inescapable quality for me. Ever since childhood, whenever I hear it read, I have a feeling first of sadness and then of alarm. The sadness comes from the fact that it is a story of someone who believes he has everything, but actually he has nothing. Instances of self-deception on such a grand scale are highly unsettling to behold – the foolish person who prattles on convinced that he is saying something of value when in fact what he has to say is no more than a collection of tired clichés; the joke-teller who thinks she is the fount of wit but who, in reality, is a boring recycler of stale stories. Alarm then arises when it all begins to bend back upon the beholder and the possibility dawns that one might oneself be subject to similar illusions. We may then, with Robert Burns, wish for the gift to see ourselves as others see us or, better still, as God sees us.

Nowhere is the capacity for self-delusion more insidiously attractive than when it operates to distract us from the great certainty of death. The average weekend colour supplement sets out to persuade us of the glamour of possessions and the status and satisfaction that come from having them. Build bigger barns (have a handy loan to do so – take the waiting out of wanting), stuff them full of goods, and then relax, eat, drink and be merry. It would be a bold guest at such a party who could say, 'You fool! This very night your soul is demanded of you.' Yet the reality is that we live in a world of transience, and nothing will be ours for ever that is simply purchased out of a luxuriously illustrated colour catalogue. One might think of those medieval images of the Dance of Death. They depict a time of plague, and people are seeking to distract themselves with the pleasures of a grand ball. Yet among the richly apparelled revellers there is a skeleton figure inside one of the sumptuous robes. Death simply cannot be kept at bay by pleasure-seeking.

By now I may seem like a really grim killjoy. Yet I am not advocating a life of bread and water, with clothes bought only from the nearly new shop, nor am I trying to persuade you, as some people did in the seventeenth century, to sleep in your shroud and use your future coffin as your bed. All I hope for myself and for you is that we shall be able to come to terms with reality, both the real value of the gifts that we receive in life, whether they are gifts of friendship, or the pleasure of a good meal with some decent wine, or the occasional satisfaction of being smartly dressed for a special event, and also with the reality that these things will one day pass away from us, as our lives close in the death that is our inevitable destiny.

If we are able to use this life in order to know something of the God whose steadfast love is the guarantee of a destiny beyond death, then we shall be able to accept with gratitude the gifts we receive without feeling that they must be artificially multiplied beyond measure and clung to with a greedy appetite, and also to face the fact of mortality without resentment or despair. Above all, we shall be able to be clear-eyed and honest, not living in the fool's paradise of conspicuous consumption. In the great vision that begins the book of Revelation, the risen Christ speaks to the church of Laodicea and says, 'You say, "I am rich, I have prospered, and I need nothing." You do not realize that you are wretched, pitiable, poor, blind and naked. Therefore I counsel you to buy from me gold refined by fire so that you may be rich; and white robes to clothe you and keep the shame of your nakedness from being seen; and salve to anoint your eyes so that you may see' (Revelation 3.17–18). May God deliver us from illusion and lead us into the true riches of eternal life; may God purify our desires.

Prayer
O almighty God, who alone canst order the unruly wills and affections of sinful men; Grant unto thy people, that they may love the thing which thou commandest, and desire that which thou dost promise; that so, among the sundry and manifold changes of the world, our hearts may surely there be fixed, where true joys are to be found: through Jesus Christ our Lord.

(*Book of Common Prayer*, 1662)

Friday: Individual destiny

> *Peter turned and saw the disciple whom Jesus loved following them ... When Peter saw him, he said to Jesus, 'Lord, what about him?' Jesus said to him, 'If it is my will that he remain until I come, what is that to you? Follow me!'*

(John 21.20–22)

This short gospel scene follows immediately after a longer conversation between Peter and the risen Christ in which the one who had three times denied Jesus is led to confess three times, 'Lord, you know that I love you.' Peter is then told that later in life he will be called to submit to those 'who will take you where you do not wish to go'. The writer of the

Gospel comments that this saying indicated 'the kind of death by which he would glorify God'. Ancient tradition tells us that this prophecy was fulfilled when Peter was crucified in Rome during Nero's persecution of the Christians there.

Now Peter turns and sees 'the disciple whom Jesus loved' (whom we shall call John) following along behind. His curiosity leads him to ask what will be that disciple's destiny. In effect he gets the answer from Jesus that he should mind his own business. Tradition suggests that John the Apostle lived into extreme old age and died peacefully, probably in Ephesus. It seems that the destinies of these two apostles, Peter and John, were to prove to be very different.

When we think of the role of death in people's lives, we continually encounter the mystery of individual human destiny. Some have serene lives, ending in honoured old age; others die sadly prematurely, as it seems, with what one might consider to be only half a lifetime's work completed. There often does not seem to be rhyme or reason in these matters, and they cause us great perplexity.

We face similar ambiguities when we pray for those who are seriously ill. Our wish for them is healing, which in its truest sense means the attainment of wholeness in the experience that has come upon them. If we reflect deeply enough, we can see that this gift might take the form of physical recovery, or it might take the form of grace given to accept the imminent destiny of death. No one can predict beforehand which it will prove to be, and only those closely involved have the right to say afterwards whether, and in what form, healing was actually given.

David Watson was a noted charismatic Christian leader, an evangelist whose preaching had helped many thousands of people to hear and respond to the gospel of Christ. In middle life, at the height of his powers and activity as it seemed, he discovered out of the blue that he had inoperable cancer. Of course, very many people began to pray for God's healing for him. David himself began to write a book, subsequently published under the title *Fear No Evil* (Hodder and Stoughton), which was a kind of diary of his experiences. If one reads that book, it is clear that it was originally expected to turn out to be an account of God's miraculous restoration of physical health. In fact, as the book progresses, it turns into a most moving and inspiring account of how David Watson was able to accept the fact that an early death was to be God's destiny for him. The honesty and integrity of the account is profoundly impressive and helpful to the reader. What might have seemed to be an inexplicable and bitter happening had borne much strange fruit.

When we think about suffering, and when we think about death, we cannot escape from wrestling with the mysteries of individual human destiny. Those who are able to face these matters with the clear-eyed trust of a David Watson, are those who are able to say with St Paul,

> For I am convinced that neither death, nor life, nor angels, nor rulers, nor things present, nor things to come, nor powers, nor height, nor depth, nor anything else in all creation, will be able to separate us from the love of God in Christ Jesus our Lord.
>
> (Romans 8.38–39)

May God set such a steadfast hope in our hearts also.

Prayer
Lord, in the strangenesses and perplexities of life, help us to hold fast to you and to trust in your steadfast love that death itself cannot defeat.

Saturday: Sorrow

> *But we do not want you to be uninformed, brothers and sisters, about those who have died, so that you may not grieve as others do who have no hope.*
>
> *He said, 'Where have you laid him?' They said to him, 'Lord, come and see.' Jesus began to weep.*
>
> (1 Thessalonians 4.13; John 11.34–35)

Paul reminds bereaved Thessalonians that in Christ they have the hope of there being a destiny beyond death. Well, that's all right then, isn't it? Actually, it's a bit more complicated than that.

It is inspiring to be at a funeral where those centrally concerned embrace the Christian hope of the life of the world to come, so that the service can have a strong element of celebration and gratitude for the life of the one who has died, in the conviction that the good things thus recalled are not lost, but they are safe in God's keeping. Yet sorrow can properly be part of that funeral service also. We can see that from this extraordinary little incident in the gospel story of the raising of Lazarus. Jesus is on his way to call his friend out of the tomb and back into this life, yet he also shares in the sorrow of the grieving relatives. 'Jesus began to weep.'

Death is real even if, before the ultimate reality of God, we can see that it is not an absolute reality, a total annihilation. Death marks an end, resulting in a real separation – even if it is not a permanent one – at which we naturally feel sorrow. Think of a family in the nineteenth century, one of whose members is about to emigrate to Australia. The family left behind believes that good prospects lie ahead for the one who is leaving them, but they also know that they will never see them again. Gladness at the promise of the new country must have been mixed with sorrow that the one departing will never be in the old country again. So it is for us when death parts us from those whom we love in this life.

Coming to terms with the separation of bereavement is a lengthy process. It is certainly not accomplished in the few days that elapse between a death and a funeral. In fact, often the loss suffered only really begins to dawn in the months that follow, when life returns to 'normal', but with a very big unfilled gap in it. It is important, as much as we can, to carry on our support for the bereaved well beyond the day of the funeral.

A parish priest who visits a widow or a widower will very often be asked, 'Will I see my husband/wife again?' I have always felt able to say, 'Yes', because I truly believe that nothing of good is lost in the Lord, and some of our greatest goods lie in our closest relationships. In God's mercy, they must surely be restored and fulfilled in the life of the world to come.

One way in which we can keep in spiritual touch with those who have died and who are dear to us, is through prayer. Of course, it is true that Christians have disagreed about prayers for the dead. Quite a lot of this controversy derived from reactions to abuses of the idea in pre-Reformation times, when the notion was touted that prayers or masses for the dead could be used as a kind of handy earthly influence to advance our friends in the heavenly realm. The rejection of these unedifying excesses should not imply rejection of the idea that in Christ there is a prayerful solidarity between those alive on earth and those whose earthly life is over. On the contrary, this way of thinking about and experiencing the communion of saints can be of real value and comfort to those who sorrow.

Prayer

O Lord our God, from whom neither life nor death can separate those who trust in thy love, and whose love holds in remembrance thy children of this world and the next; so unite us to thyself that in fellowship with thee we may always be united to our loved ones, whether here or there; give us courage, constancy and hope; through him who died and was buried and rose again for us, Jesus Christ our Lord.

(Archbishop William Temple)

Advent 2

Unseen realities

So we do not lose heart. Even though our outer nature is wasting away, our inner nature is being renewed day by day. For this slight momentary affliction is preparing us for an eternal weight of glory beyond all measure, because we look not at what can be seen but at what cannot be seen; for what can be seen is temporary, but what cannot be seen is eternal.

(2 Corinthians 4.16–18)

For half my working life I was a theoretical physicist, seeking to use mathematics to understand the fundamental nature of matter. I was lucky, for it turned out that those 25 years coincided with a very interesting period in my subject. It was a time when physicists encountered and understood a new level in the structure of matter. This came about through the discovery of constituents called quarks.

The way it happened was like this: The first step was to recognize that the particles that we knew about already could be arranged in some simple patterns, and that these patterns were just those that could be interpreted as showing that these known objects were made out of combinations of some more basic entities, the quarks. That was very suggestive, but by itself it did not settle the matter. The second step was to do some experiments in which very fast projectiles were fired at the known particles. It was discovered that these missiles sometimes bounced back, just as if they were hitting something harder and smaller inside the target particles. When you analysed in detail what was going on in these experiments, the properties of these little hard bits turned out to be just those that corresponded to their being quarks. They just had to be there, rattling around inside!

It was a very important discovery, and the leaders of the investigation got their Nobel Prizes. Yet no one has ever seen an individual quark. Somehow it seems that they are so tightly lodged inside the particles that they make up that even the strongest impact is not enough to knock them out. So should those distinguished physicists give back their Nobel Prizes? Not at all! We believe in quarks not because we have seen them sitting there on their own, but because that belief makes sense of so much experience that we can observe directly.

Why do I tell this somewhat complicated, and perhaps somewhat mysterious, story from elementary particle physics? To show you that it is perfectly natural for scientists to believe in unseen realities, provided that belief makes sense of great swathes of seen experience. I think the same is true of belief in the greatest unseen reality of all – God. No one has seen God directly, but Christian belief makes sense of great swathes of spiritual experience, both that recorded in the Bible and that testified to down the centuries by the witness of the Church. In this respect science and religion are really quite close to each other.

In our passage for today, St Paul is reminding the Corinthians of the unseen reality of the hope of eternal life, the 'weight of glory beyond all measure', that God has prepared for those who accept the offer of divine love. When Paul was writing, he certainly did not see that glory directly – in fact he makes it clear in his letter that life was pretty tough for him and for some of his readers. Yet they had sufficient direct experience of the grace given them from God the Father, and the hope given them through the risen Christ, and sufficient knowledge of the Spirit at work in their hearts, to be able to believe that God would indeed bring them into that final inheritance of glory.

'Seeing is believing', people say, but our lives would be greatly impoverished if we only trusted in what appears before our eyes. The loving commitment that a parent has to a child, or two people to each other in the lifelong partnership of marriage, are not things that can be held up for inspection, for they are present in a veiled form, expressed through a consistent attitude to life. Faith in those dear to us, or faith in the God who cares for us, are both a form of trust in unseen reality. These beliefs are not fantasies of wishful thinking, for we have reasons for trusting that they are true, but they are not items that can simply be looked at and directly checked.

Advent is a time to think about the unseen realities lying beneath the surface of life but providing its present foundation and its future hope. 'What can be seen is temporary, but what cannot be seen is eternal.'

Prayer
O God, the protector of all that trust in thee, without whom nothing is strong, nothing is holy; Increase and multiply upon us thy mercy; that, thou being our ruler and guide, we may so pass through things temporal, that we finally lose not the things eternal: Grant this heavenly Father, for Jesus Christ's sake our Lord.

(*Book of Common Prayer*, 1662)

Monday: Judgement

And this is the judgement, that the light has come into the world, and people loved darkness rather than light because their deeds were evil. For all who do evil hate the light and do not come to the light, so that their deeds may not be exposed. But those who do what is true come to the light, so that it may be clearly seen that their deeds have been done in God.

(John 3.19–21)

There have been centuries in which people have been very concerned and fearful about God's judgement on sinners. This century is certainly not one of them. Much more characteristic of modern attitudes were the words of a dissolute poet on his deathbed. When asked if he did not fear judgement to come, he replied, 'Oh, God will forgive me – that's his line of business.'

I think there are two main reasons why judgement has become so neglected a theme today. One is that people have succumbed to a sentimental understanding of divine love, failing to perceive adequately the moral seriousness that is part of God's holy nature. The fatherhood of God is not the indulgence of a foolishly doting parent who colludes with the harmful behaviour of a spoilt child. God cares too much for the welfare of creatures to behave in that unwise kind of way. It matters how we form our characters, something which we do through the way in which we live our lives. The poet's moral flippancy was spiritually damaging.

An opposite difficulty about the idea of judgement arose from the way in which it sometimes was proclaimed within the Christian community. All too often the picture given was one of an irascible tyrant quick to condemn, a kind of celestial Judge Jeffreys. The fear of a terrible judgement was invoked by hell-fire preachers as if it were the way to drive frightened sinners into the arms of a loving God. It would be impossible to deny that there is scriptural imagery to which an appeal could be made in this way. The book of Revelation comes particularly to mind, but it is important to recognize the style in which that strange book is written. It is packed with pungent symbolism, much of it with something of the vividness and crudity of an animated cartoon. Pictures of eternal death, and of the sulphurous lake of fire, are certainly powerful images reinforcing a message of moral seriousness, but they are dangerous images with which to play in isolation from the rest of scripture.

Today's passage from St John's Gospel presents us with a different way of thinking about judgement. If we understand it rightly, it is equally stern in its moral seriousness, but it is untainted by any suspicion of sadistic involvement with punishment for punishment's sake. 'This is the judgement, that light came into the world, and people loved darkness rather than light because their deeds were evil.'

The root thought here is that judgement is not imposed

arbitrarily from without, but we experience it from within because it centres on our reaction to reality ('light'), our response to the ways that things truly are. Confronted with reality – including the reality of who we are and what we have done – we can either turn towards the light, acccepting the painful fact of evil done as the first step through which we may begin to be changed and conformed to the holy reality of God's will; or we can turn away from the light into the darkness of ourselves, as we cling to the delusion that there is nothing really the matter with us.

Understood in this way as an opening up to the truth, judgement is a hopeful word. Reality may be painful, and we may only be able to bear a little of it at a time, but facing it is the only possible route to true fulfilment. There is no future in illusion. In human society, the best penal practice aims to help criminals confront the reality of their crimes and the damage done by them, and then to help them to build a new way of life, in a state no longer distorted by the legacy of the past. Human success in this endeavour is inevitably patchy, and it certainly requires the willing cooperation of the persons involved. God too looks to us for our cooperation, for our acceptance of the resources of grace, for salvation will never be imposed upon us against our will by irresistible divine fiat. Judgement is a part of that process of acceptance, and in the course of it we can know that we are not meeting with a hanging Judge, but with the One who longs for us to enter purified into our full inheritance as children of God.

Prayer

O God, who makest us glad with the yearly remembrance of the birth of thy only Son Jesus Christ: Grant that as we joyfully receive him for our Redeemer, so we may have sure confidence to behold him when he shall come to be our Judge: who liveth and reigneth with thee and the Holy Ghost, ever one God, world without end.

(*Gelasian Sacramentary*, eighth century)

Tuesday: The distortive effects of sin

So I find it to be a law that when I want to do what is good, evil lies close at hand. For I delight in the law of God in my inmost self, but I see in my members another law at war with the law of my mind, making me captive to the law of sin that dwells in my members.

(Romans 7.21–23)

Something has gone wrong with humanity. Despite great achievements and noble heroism, history is also the tale of wars, persecutions and exploitation. There is a slantedness in human life that distorts our actions and frustrates our best intentions. I am not just talking about people of a spectacularly evil way of life – mass murderers or ruthless defrauders of the poor – but of what is part of the everyday experience of all of us, as we can see if we stop to review our lives. This slantedness takes many forms: that spiteful word spoken out of resentment, or out of a desire to hurt as a part of petty revenge; the shabby deal that enabled us to get away with giving someone less than was their due; the compromise that let us dodge the facing of a painful truth; a betrayal of trust to gain an illicit advantage. Why are things like that? Where does it all come from?

The Christian diagnosis is that the origin of this state of affairs lies in the distortive effects of sin. Notice the singular, for it is important to recognize the difference between sin and sins. The latter are the particular deeds, such as those I have been talking about, which fall short of right behaviour. Some of these can be fairly mild (irritability when stressed) and others terribly destructive (persistent hatred of someone). Yet they are all simply symptoms of an underlying spiritual disease, and it is that disease which is sin itself. We have thought about it already when we considered the meaning of the Fall, for sin is the state of chosen alienation from God, when we turn into ourselves and away from God, because we want to have our own way and to grasp our chosen gratifications without any restraint from outside ourselves. This self-

centred strategy proves to be a disastrous mistake, not
because it upsets a God who simply wants us to be subservient slaves, but because it denies the fact that true
human freedom comes from accepting our status as creatures who need to look to our creator as the source of the
fullness of life. As the learned say, human beings in their
true nature are heteronymous (dependent on Another),
and not autonymous (as if we really were the masters of our
fate and the captains of our soul, owing nothing to anyone).

The distortive effects of sin can turn a country's liberator
into its next tyrant. A famous American theologian,
Reinhold Niebuhr, once said that the doctrine of sin was the
only Christian belief that was directly verifiable by observa-
tion – just look around you at the world, or within the depths
of your own heart, and you will see what it is all about. Sin is
a disease from which we all suffer, even the greatest of the
saints. Today's short passage shows us St Paul being aston-
ishingly frank about its effects in his own life. In fact, the
greatest saints have often been those whose acute spiritual
perception had made them most aware of the destructive
force of sin.

This fact makes it all the more surprising, at first sight, that
the Gospel records never indicate the presence of this feeling
in Jesus himself. It is part of traditional Christian belief that
Jesus was actually sinless – not free from temptation, think
of the wilderness (Matthew 4.1–11) and Gethsemane (Matthew 26.36–46) – but free from the distortive effects of sin.
Because he was tempted, he understands what can decoy us
into sin; because he himself did not succumb to temptation,
he is able to help us out of our alienation and back into a
right relationship with God his Father. After the confession of
his own weakness, Paul goes on to say, 'Wretched man that I
am! Who will rescue me from this body of death? Thanks be
to God through Jesus Christ our Lord!' (Romans 7.24–25).

Prayer
Almighty and everlasting God, who hatest nothing that thou
has made, and dost forgive the sins of all them that are

penitent; Create and make in us new and contrite hearts, that we worthily lamenting our sins, and acknowledging our wretchedness, may obtain of thee, the God of all mercy, perfect remission and forgiveness; through Jesus Christ our Lord.

(Ash Wednesday, *Book of Common Prayer*, 1662)

Wednesday: Divine wrath

Therefore God gave them up in the lusts of their hearts to impurity, to the degrading of their bodies among themselves, because they exchanged the truth about God for a lie and worshipped and served the creature rather than the creator, who is blessed for ever! Amen.

(Romans 1.24–25)

Today's subject is one that is very easily misunderstood. The phrase 'the wrath of God' all too readily conjures up the picture of a testy Jehovah, a God who is easily upset and who, when thus put out, hurls a hasty and destructive punishment upon the disobedient offender. The image is that of the Celestial Tyrant who must be placated at all costs. I remember talking once to a historian who had made a particular study of life in the Soviet Union under Stalin. He told me that the reason there was never a real move to topple the dictator was simply the fear of what would happen to the person who was the first to shift an inch out of line. There are stories of Stalin making a speech after which the applause seemed endless, just because of the anxiety that the first to stop clapping would next day be on the way to the Gulag.

So is God like that? Of course not. How could the God whose nature is love be the Potentate whose irritable anger all must fear? Does that then mean that the idea of the wrath of God is one that we should get rid of as soon as possible? I do not think so, because behind the phrase when it is rightly understood, there lies a fact of great significance. It is simply this: deeds have consequences.

God is not the Tyrant whose will is imposed on all through

the exercise of irresistible power and the force of fear. Quite the contrary, for the gift of the God of love is the gift of freedom to those who are the objects of that divine love. We are allowed to be ourselves and to make our own decisions. But just as God allows human freedom and does not arbitrarily curtail it, so also God will not arbitrarily intervene to set aside the consequences that flow from the exercise of that freedom. 'Do not be deceived; God is not mocked, for you reap whatever you sow' (Galatians 6.7). That is the wrath of God – not the lashing out of an angry deity, but the moral seriousness of God's creation in which deeds have their consequences. The selfish person who takes but never gives, will end life in unloved isolation. The parent whose relentless pursuit of personal ambition results in the neglect of all else, including the needs of the children, will not enjoy the mature satisfactions of family life.

In the short passage from Romans, Paul tells us that God gives up to impurity and degradation those who exchange the truth for a lie. It is a picture whose sober reality is more chillingly tragic than any image of blazing divine anger could ever be. We may be sure that this giving up is not an act of impatience but an act of sadness for God. It is the feeling that the father of the prodigal son must have had when that young man took his share of the inheritance and used his freedom to go off into the far country and squander these resources in wasteful and profitless living. Yet when the prodigal 'came to himself' (began to see the truth of the matter and to abandon the life of the lie), that father was not only prepared to receive him back into the family home, but actually ran to meet him on his long-awaited return. We cannot believe less of the God and Father of our Lord Jesus Christ. The wrath of God is real, but so is God's steadfast and unchanging love. The divine purpose is not to punish us but to purify us.

Prayer

> Create in me a clean heart, O God,
>   and put a right spirit within me.
> Do not cast me away from your presence,
>   and do not take your holy spirit from me.
> Restore to me the joy of your salvation,
>   and sustain in me a willing spirit.
>
> (Psalm 51.10–12)

Thursday: The coming of the hidden Christ

Then the righteous will answer him, 'Lord, when was it that we saw you hungry and gave you food, or thirsty and gave you something to drink? And when was it that we saw you a stranger and welcomed you, or naked and gave you clothing?' ... And the king will answer them, 'Truly I tell you, just as you did it to the least of these who are members of my family, you did it to me.' ... Then they also will answer, 'Lord, when was it that we saw you hungry or thirsty or a stranger or naked or sick or in prison, and did not take care of you?' Then he will answer them, 'Truly I tell you, just as you did not do it to one of the least of these, you did not do it to me.'

(Matthew 25.37–38, 40, 44–45)

In Palestine in Jesus' day, it was common for there to be mixed herds of sheep and goats, but at the end of the day the shepherd had to separate the two, since the goats were less hardy and they had to be protected from the night-time cold in a way not necessary for the tougher and more valuable sheep. Jesus uses this image in speaking about judgement. His parable of the sheep and goats presents us with a picture of the final Assize in which the criterion on which the verdict is based focuses on deeds of compassion and mercy. The blessed have shown pity to those in need, but the ones who are condemned are those whose hardness of heart has lead them to neglect the poor.

What makes this parable so haunting is that both groups

of people, both the sheep and the goats, were totally unaware of what was happening. The righteous 'sheep' are mystified when they are told that they have shown mercy to the Lord himself. 'Lord, when did we see you … ?' They are told that 'just as you did it to the least of these who are members of my family, you did it to me'. Not only is no good deed ever wasted, but it is Christ-centred in its effect: 'For truly I tell you, whoever gives you a cup of water to drink because you bear the name of Christ will by no means lose the reward' (Mark 9.41).

Equally, the 'goats' did not realize who it was they were neglecting in their disregard of the poor. We can imagine them saying, 'Of course, Lord, if we had known it was *you*, we would have been only too pleased to do something. In fact, we would have got out the red carpet right away. Nothing would have been too much trouble. But we thought it was only that funny old bag lady who is so embarrassing and makes such a nuisance of herself with all her begging and scavenging. Or we thought it was just that tiresome, moody teenager who wanted our attention when we had something far more interesting to do. Or it was those famine victims somewhere in Africa, who certainly look pretty pathetic in the short clips on television, but who are too far away for us to be really concerned about them.' To the goats, and to us, Christ says, 'Truly I tell you, just as you did not do it to one of the least of these, you did not do it to me.'

In Advent, we think about the coming of Christ, particularly that first coming at Bethlehem and that final coming at the end of the age to judge the world. But the truth of the matter is that Christ comes to us everyday, anonymously in the people in need who cross our path. In connection with the greeting of strangers, the Rule of St Benedict instructs the monks, 'All guests are to be received as Christ himself.'

We need to pray for grace to perceive the needs of those we encounter for, although that need will sometimes be obvious, quite often it will be veiled and some power of spiritual perception will be required to discern what it is and to understand its true character. We need also to pray for the wisdom and generosity that will enable us to play our part in the meeting of that need. Even so, come Lord Jesus.

Prayer
Heavenly Father, whose Son taught us that what we do for the least of his brothers and sisters, we do for him: Help us to see him and to serve him in the need of those who cross our paths, and in all the suffering people of the world.

Friday: Purgation, not destruction

> *For no one can lay any foundation other than the one that has been laid; that foundation is Jesus Christ. Now if anyone builds on the foundation with gold, silver, precious stones, wood, hay straw – the work of each builder will become visible, for the Day will disclose it, because it will be revealed with fire, and the fire will test what sort of work each has done. If what has been built on the foundation survives, the builder will receive a reward. If the work is burned, the builder will suffer loss; the builder will be saved, but only as through fire.*
>
> (1 Corinthians 3.11–15)

If judgement is encounter with reality, it is a hopeful prospect, since opening up to truth is much better than remaining in deceptive illusion. Nevertheless, judgement may prove to be a painful process. We often cling to fantasies and deceive ourselves about our real nature, so that it will not be costless for us to let go of the idols to which we cling. Yet a process of purgation will surely be an indispensable preliminary before we are ready to approach closer to the presence of the holy reality of God. I therefore think that some form of belief in purgatory is an essential part of an adequate understanding of the Christian hope for the life that awaits us beyond death.

Many readers may feel something of an instinctive disinclination to accept this claim. Purgatory got a bad name during the events that led up to the Reformation and certainly no one today would want to believe the grossly misleading idea that ritual acts, or payments made in this life, could buy favourable treatment in the life to come and so ease the way of the privileged into heaven. A totally different concept is given us by St Paul, whose picture of purgation is one in which the dross of our lives is burnt away in order that the good may remain untainted.

Paul's chosen metaphor is of cleansing by fire, but it is not the torturing flames of the executioner's pyre or the destructive flames of wholesale conflagration that he has in mind. Instead it is something like the refiner's fire, that in the crucible brings to light the gold that had been concealed by the base metal that mingled with it. That there should be such a process of purification is entirely consistent with what we know about the way in which God works. When we think of the history of creation – the 14 billion year history of the universe and the three to four billion year evolving history of life on earth – we see that God is patient and subtle, by no means a God in a hurry. When we think about God's nature as love, we can see that this is how we would expect the divine purpose to be fulfilled, by the gentle unfolding of process rather than by the overwhelming operation of instantaneous power.

There is another image of purgation that I find helpful and moving. It comes in Dante's great poem *The Divine Comedy*, whose second volume is devoted to Purgatory. The picture is that of a great mountain that links earth to heaven and which has seven levels, each associated with one of the seven deadly sins. As people progress slowly but steadily up this spiritual slope, they are purified from each deadly sin in turn as they move on from one level to the next. When someone makes this transition, the whole mountain shakes with the sound of Alleluias, as all rejoice at the spiritual progress being made. The idea of purification, and the concept of purgatory that goes with it, are essential components in the Christian hope for the life of the world to come.

Prayer
O God, may the fire of your Holy Spirit consume in us all that displeases you, and kindle in our hearts a burning zeal for the service of your kingdom, through Jesus Christ our Lord.

Saturday: Do not judge

Do not judge, so that you may not be judged. For with the judgement you make you will be judged, and the measure you give will be the measure you get. Why do you see the speck in your neighbour's eye, but do not notice the log in your own eye?

(Matthew 7.1–3)

If judgement is encounter with reality, then uttering the verdict of judgement belongs to God, for only divine knowledge has the clarity truly to see things as they are. Our moral vision is subject to cloudiness, distortion and tricks of perspective. Hence Jesus' warning, 'Do not judge'.

So often we are able to see only a little of what is going on. 'So-and-so was really dull and slow today, dragging their feet and scarcely doing even half a day's work. What a slacker.' Hidden from us is So-and-so's secret anxiety about the referral to the cancer clinic, that has induced the heaviness of heart that made it hard for them to concentrate on their work.

So often our criticism of others is a projection of the self-criticism that we feel within ourselves, but which we are unable to face honestly. It is so easy to recognize in others the faults that we ourselves possess. Let us concentrate on that speck in the neighbour's eye, and try to forget about that log in our own eye.

So often we try to purchase a spurious self-esteem by diminishing the attainments of others. Our envy of the social success of our generous and witty neighbour leads us to devalue that generosity as spendthrift and that wit as verbal showing off. Of course, that sometimes might be true, but we need to beware of the meanness of spirit that is unable to recognize the good in others, a strategy that we adopt in order to maintain our internal self-congratulation untroubled by the fact that their gifts exceed ours in some respects.

On another occasion, Jesus made the same kind of point about the dangers of human judging by his vivid parable of the Pharisee and the tax-collector in the temple (Luke 18.9–14). The Pharisee is a man with many admirable practices, good living and scrupulous in his religious duties. But it seems that it is not enough for him to thank God for the character of life that his upbringing has enabled him to attain. All that has to be inflated and turned into self-congratulation by indulging in judging his neighbour, the tax-collector who is apparently so gratifyingly unworthy. 'God, I thank you that I am not like other people ...' Then there is the tax-collector himself, a despised member of society whose profession was riddled with corrupt and extortionate practices. In terms of probity and good to the community, the Pharisee seems to win hands down. But the tax-collector has something vital that his superior neighbour lacks: the honesty to see himself as he is and to acknowledge his need of God's grace: 'God be merciful to me, a sinner!' Jesus tells us that 'this man went down to his home justified rather than the other'.

The antidote to being judgemental is to be humble. Humility is not a kind of silly game in which clever people pretend that they are fools, or handsome people that they are ugly. It is simply a clear-eyed way of facing reality, of being as pleased with valuable talents when we encounter them in others, as we are grateful when we find them in ourselves. The humble gardener rejoices in the quality of the prize-winning roses, irrespective of whose garden they came from; the humble cook rejoices in the quality of the meal, no matter from whose kitchen it came.

Prayer

Give me, good Lord, a humble, lowly, quiet and peaceable mind, with all my words and all my works, and all my thoughts, to have a taste of thy holy blessed Spirit.

(Sir Thomas More)

Advent 3

John the Baptist

John the baptizer appeared in the wilderness, proclaiming a baptism of repentance for the forgiveness of sins. And people from the whole Judean countryside and all the people of Jerusalem were going out to him, and were baptized by him in the river Jordan, confessing their sins. Now John was clothed with camel's hair, with a leather belt around his waist, and he ate locusts and wild honey.
(Mark 1.4–6)

John the Baptist is a great figure in religious history. Although he appears in the pages of the New Testament, his real role is the completion of the great prophetic tradition that is so significant a part of the testimony of the Hebrew Bible (the Jewish writings that Christians call the Old Testament). That prophetic movement had a brief further flowering after the Jews returned from exile in Babylon and the temple was rebuilt. Prophets such as Haggai and Zechariah proclaimed that there would be a restoration of former glory, but this did not fully come about and the voice of prophecy then fell silent for several centuries, in the course of which external powers, such as Persia, Alexander's empire and Rome, ruled over Judea. All that the rabbinic thinkers seemed to be able to hear was a faint divine whisper. The clear voice of God no longer echoed in the land.

Then, all of a sudden, John the Baptist appeared. He was a striking sight, though not someone whom you would readily ask in for a cup of tea if he knocked on your door. He came out of the desert and he was uncouthly dressed, 'clothed in camel's hair'. That, actually, was a clue for those who had the wit to make it out, for the way in which Mark describes John closely parallels the way in which Elijah is described in 2 Kings 1.8. Elijah was the first great prophetic figure in Israel's history; John was to be the last.

The Baptist was a charismatic preacher, who drew large crowds – the Billy Graham of his day. His talk was straight and uncompromising, for he conveyed a stern message: 'Repent, for the kingdom of heaven has come near' (Matthew 3.2). There was nothing ingratiating about John: 'You brood of vipers! Who warned you to flee from the wrath to come?' (Matthew 3.7). What was particularly distinctive about him was what gave rise to his nickname. John required those who repented of their sinful ways to show their desire for a changed and cleansed life by undergoing immersion in the river Jordan. We shall think some more about this when we come to consider how Jesus himself was baptized by John (January 7).

Not only was John the last of the Hebrew prophets, his ministry also anticipated a great new work that God was about to bring about. John was very clear about this. 'The one who is more powerful than I is coming after me … I have baptized you with water; but he will baptize you with the Holy Spirit' (Mark 1.7–8). Matthew (3.14) and John (1.32–34) both tell us that when Jesus of Nazareth came to John, the Baptist recognized that here was the one for whom he had been preparing the way.

John's character is marked by integrity and strength, but even he could waver and be uncertain under the effect of persecution. Unjustly imprisoned by Herod, he began to wonder what God was actually up to and whether he might not have been mistaken about the significance of Jesus. So, from prison, John sent messengers to Jesus to ask him what is going on: 'Are you the one who is to come, or are we to await for another?' (Matthew 11.2). Jesus does not get into an argument, but he simply points John and the messengers to the good deeds that he is performing. Where there is healing and liberation, there is truly the kingdom of God present in power. Shortly after receiving this reply, John's life ends in martyrdom, when a rash and drunken Herod is forced into executing him in order to placate a malicious woman and in order not to lose face before the courtiers with whom he has been carousing (Mark 6.17–29).

Jesus said of John that 'among those born of woman no one has arisen greater than he', but he also went on to say, 'yet the least in the kingdom of heaven is greater than he' (Matthew 11.11). It has been given to us to see the fullness of Christ's glory, of which John had only been able to catch an anticipatory glimpse.

Prayer

Almighty God, by whose providence your servant John the Baptist was wonderfully born, and sent to prepare the way of your Son our saviour by the preaching of repentance, lead us to repent according to his preaching and, after his example, constantly to speak the truth, boldly to rebuke vice, and patiently to suffer for the truth's sake; through Jesus Christ your Son our Lord, who is alive and reigns with you in the unity of the Holy Spirit, one God, now and for ever.

(Collect for the Birth of St John the Baptist)

Monday: Heaven

'And as for the dead being raised, have you not read in the book of Moses, in the story about the bush, how God said to him, "I am the God of Abraham, the God of Isaac and the God of Jacob"? He is God not of the dead, but of the living; you are quite wrong.'

(Mark 12.26–27)

(It would actually be a good idea to read the whole of Mark 12.18–27.) It is part of the Advent hope that we have a destiny awaiting us beyond our deaths. If we accept the fullness of the new life that will then be set before us, we shall enter into the life of heaven. As we begin to think about what that could mean, we need first to consider what could be the ground for the hope of a life beyond death. Today's short passage is one of the most important in the New Testament in helping us to deal with that question.

Jesus is engaged in a discussion with the Sadducees. They were a small but very influential sect in the Judaism of the time. The Sadducees controlled the worship of the temple, and they were continually engaged in a delicate balancing act with the occupying Roman power, as they tried to ensure that the temple worship would be maintained free from external interference. Theologically the Sadducees were very conservative. Out of all the writings preserved in the Hebrew Bible, they only accepted as truly authoritative the first five books, Genesis to Deuteronomy. These constituted the *Torah*, the law, the absolute centre of Jewish scripture. The Sadducees did not feel that they found in these five books any clear promise of a destiny beyond death, and so they rejected that belief altogether.

They come to Jesus to argue the point, and they put their case in a very ingenious way. There was this woman whose husband died without their having had any children. In Jewish law there was an obligation on the next brother to marry the widow in order, if possible, that there should be children born to perpetuate the dead man's memory. But that brother also died without issue and the responsibility then passed on to the next in line. Unfortunately, he died too, and so on through all the seven brothers, without any child having been born. Finally, the woman herself died. Now comes the punchline: 'In the resurrection whose wife will she be?' (v. 23). In other words, if there were to be a life after death, how would it be possible to sort out all the messy and confused entanglements left over from this life?

It is a characteristically clever Jewish conundrum, but Jesus, as he so often did, cuts through the superficial issue to get to the heart of the matter. He takes those Sadducees back to Exodus 3.6, which, of course, was a verse whose authority they had to take very seriously. At the burning bush, God says to Moses, 'I am the God of your father, the God of Abraham, the God of Isaac and the God of Jacob.' A very important conclusion then follows from these solemn words. God is not someone who cares for a person today and then cannot be bothered about that person tomorrow. God's character is that of faithful and steadfast love (there is an important word for this in Hebrew: *hesed*). Therefore, if the patriarchs mattered to God once – and they certainly did – they must matter to God for ever. Jesus says, 'He is the God not of the dead, but of the living; you are quite wrong.' The error is to fail to take the everlasting faithfulness of God with absolute seriousness.

Jesus' argument is powerful and convincing. We have no simply natural expectation of a destiny beyond death. As far as science, or any other purely human form of knowledge can tell us, death is the end. But death is not the ultimate end, because only God is ultimate. Our hope of heaven rests solely, but absolutely adequately, on the merciful faithfulness of God. If we matter to God today – and we certainly do – then we shall matter to God for ever. God is indeed the God of the living and not of the dead. In the course of this week we shall try to explore how we can understand the nature of the life of the world to come. It will be important in our discussion always to keep in mind that the ground of our hope lies in the character of God, and not in the inevitably somewhat speculative human thinking about the details of that future destiny.

For the Christian, one final point remains to be made. It is our belief that in raising Jesus from the dead the first Easter Day, God has already brought into being the full life of heaven. That is an insight of the greatest importance, but one that belongs more to a book focused on Lent and Easter than to this book with its Advent and Epiphany theme, and so we shall not pursue it in detail here, even though the resurrection of Christ can never be far from our minds when we think of the hope of a destiny beyond death.

Prayer
Blessed be the God and Father of our Lord Jesus Christ! By his great mercy he has given us a new birth into a living hope through the resurrection of Jesus Christ from the dead.

(1 Peter 1.3)

Tuesday: Continuity – The soul

For we know that if the earthly tent we live in is destroyed, we have a building from God, a house not made with hands, eternal in the heavens. For in this tent we groan, longing to be clothed with our heavenly dwelling – if indeed when we have taken it off we will not be found naked.

(2 Corinthians 5.1–3)

If hope of a destiny beyond death is to make sense, it must involve a mixture of continuity and discontinuity. There must be enough continuity with this life to ensure that it really is Abraham, Isaac and Jacob who live again in the kingdom of God and not just new characters who have been given the old names. Yet there must also be discontinuity, sufficient change to ensure that they do not merely live again in order to die again. Today we shall think about the continuity aspect of Christian hope, and tomorrow about its discontinuity aspect.

The traditional answer to what it will be that connects us in the life to come with what we are in this life, has been given in terms of the continued existence of the soul. But how are we to understand that idea? We have already seen that today it is natural to think of human beings as a kind of package deal: psychosomatic unities, as people like to say. I think that we are right to think in this way and St Paul would agree with me. Today's rather difficult passage shows him expressing a horror of being found 'naked', that is to say as a soul without a body. In this life, and in the life of heaven, human beings have to be 'clothed' with some sort of body, be it earthly or heavenly in its character. (Paul has a lot more to say about this in 1 Corinthians 15.35–49.)

What then is the soul? It is surely the 'real me', but what that can actually be is a bit of a puzzle in this life, let alone beyond it. What is it that connects me, a bald, ageing academic, with the young lad with the shock of black hair in the school photograph of 60 years ago? It is tempting to suppose that the connection lies in material continuity, as that young body changed gradually into today's elderly body, but that is really an illusion. I mentioned earlier that the matter in our bodies is changing all the time, through wear and tear, eating and drinking. We have very few atoms in our bodies today that were there even three years ago, let alone 60. Philosophers sometimes like to talk about a boat that is continually being repaired at sea, so that when it eventually comes into port again every plank in it has been replaced. Is it still the same boat that left the home port, if all its material bits and pieces have been changed in this way? I would say yes, provided that the pattern had been maintained. Of course if that had been altered, so that it had sailed out as a single hull but arrived as a catamaran, the answer would have to be no. Continuity lies in the pattern and not in the planks.

It is similar for us. The real me is not the ever-changing atoms of my body, but it is the immensely complex, information-bearing pattern in which those atoms are organized. It is that pattern that is the soul, an idea that fits in with what twenty-first-century science is beginning to discover from the study of complex systems, that information is as fundamental a category as energy.

This concept of the soul as informational pattern is quite an old one. Aristotle believed something like that, and so did the great medieval theologian Thomas Aquinas. I believe that we should think this way too. If this is right, it follows that the soul, in itself, is not immortal. When I die, the pattern that is me will dissolve with the decay of my body. But it is a perfectly credible and sensible hope that God will remember that pattern – hold it in the divine memory after its natural decay – and then rebuild it when I am resurrected into the life of the world to come. Once again we are reminded of a central truth, that the true ground for hope of a destiny beyond death lies solely in the everlasting faithfulness of God.

On the Monday of Advent 1 we thought that death will be our final act of commitment into the hands of a loving God. I would like us today to repeat the prayer that we used on that occasion.

Prayer

> Still let me prove thy perfect will,
>   my acts of faith and love repeat;
> till death thine endless mercies seal,
>   and make the sacrifice complete.
>   (Charles Wesley)

Wednesday: Discontinuity – The new creation

And I heard a loud voice from the throne saying, 'See the home of God is among mortals. He will dwell with them; they will be his peoples, and God himself will be with them; he will wipe every tear from their eyes. Death will be no more; mourning and crying and pain will be no more, for the first things have passed away.'
                                   (Revelation 21.3–4)

The life of the world to come cannot just be a repeat of the life of this world with its transience and death – for what would be the point of such an encore? Instead it must be the life of what St Paul called the 'new creation' (2 Corinthians 5.17), a world of everlasting life freed from pain and sorrow, the kind of life movingly portrayed in this passage from Revelation. It will be an embodied life since – as we thought yesterday – the fact that human beings are psychosomatic unities implies that to be fully human one must have a body of some kind. But it does not have to be the same kind of body as we have at present. In fact it must be different, since the 'matter' of the world to come can no longer be in thrall to decay. Paul was right to say that 'flesh and blood cannot inherit the kingdom of God, nor does the perishable inherit the imperishable' (1 Corinthians 15.50). Here we meet head on with the discontinuity aspect of Christian hope.

There does not seem to be any reason to doubt that God can create 'matter' of this new kind, which will have the properties that will correspond to the death-free world promised in Revelation 21. But if this is so, there is a problem that we have to face squarely: If God can do that eventually, why was it not done straight away? To put it bluntly, if the new creation is going to be so wonderful, why did God bother with the old, so seemingly less than wonderful in all its change and decay? It is a very serious question, and seeking an answer will take us into quite deep theological waters.

The present creation exists at some distance from its creator. Of course, God is present to this world, but in a way that is veiled, so that creatures are not overwhelmed by the sheer power and majesty of divine reality. The God of love has given to creation the gift of being allowed to be itself, a gift reflected in the freedom granted to human beings to make their own choices, even if bad decisions can lead to disastrous consequences. Another way in which that gift of creaturely independence has been expressed is through biological evolution. Very soon after Charles Darwin had published *The Origin of Species,* an English clergyman, Charles Kingsley, grasped what was the right way to think theologically about this great scientific discovery. Kingsley said that no doubt God could have brought into being a ready-made world at a snap of the divine fingers, but the creator had chosen to do something cleverer and more valuable than that. By bringing into existence an evolving world in which life slowly developed and complexified, God had made a world *that could make itself.* Even the biological world is more than a mere divine puppet theatre. It has its own kind of freedom.

Understood in this way, an evolving creation is a greater good than a ready-made creation would be, but it is a good that has a necessary cost. Death is the inevitable price of new life in an evolutionary world, in which one generation must give way to the next. Genetic mutations, which produce new forms of life, can also produce malignancy. That there is death and suffering in the world is not due to the callousness or incompetence of its creator, but it is the inescapable shadow side of a creation making itself, existing at some distance from its creator.

God does not intend that this state of affairs should last for ever. The ultimate divine purpose is that the evolving world of the old creation shall be transformed into the everlasting world of the new creation. The latter will have a different character, since it will (through Christ, we believe – see Colossians 1.15–20) have been enabled to enter into an altogether closer connection with its creator. This old creation is a world that contains sacraments; the new creation to come will be wholly sacramental, totally suffused with the life and energies of God. That is why its 'matter' will have such different properties. Creation, it turns out, is a two-step process: first the old and only then the new. The new creation is not a second attempt by God at creating something out of nothing, but it comes from the redeeming transformation of the old creation.

Prayer

Bring us, O Lord God, at our last awakening into the house and gate of heaven, to enter into that gate and dwell in that house, where there shall be no darkness nor dazzling, but one equal light; no noise nor silence, but one equal music; no fears nor hopes, but one equal possession; no ends nor beginnings, but one equal eternity; in the habitations of thy majesty and glory, world without end.

(John Donne)

Thursday: A sacramental world

I saw no temple in the city, for its temple is the Lord God the Almighty and the Lamb. And the city has no need of sun or moon to shine on it, for the glory of God is its light and its lamp is the Lamb.

(Revelation 21.22–23)

Today we take up the theme briefly referred to at the end of yesterday: the sacramental character of the new creation. What makes heaven heavenly is that it is the realm in which the presence of God is veiled no longer, but the bright light of the divine glory shines out with the utmost clarity.

This thought is powerfully and succinctly expressed in these two verses from Revelation. For a Jewish believer there were important ways in which the presence of God could be glimpsed in this life. One was in the temple – not the place where God actually dwelt, for Solomon knew that 'Even heaven and the highest heaven cannot contain you, much less this house that I have built!' (1 Kings 8.27) – but the place where God had covenanted to be specially open to the prayers of God's people. Hence the obligation on every pious Jew to visit the temple regularly, especially at the time of Passover. There was also the witness of creation, the splendour of the sun, moon and stars that God had decreed to be lights for the earth and to be the means by which to regulate the calendar of the liturgical year (Genesis 1.14–19). Yet these signs, despite their value in the world of the old creation, will no longer be needed in the life of the new creation. In the new Jerusalem, 'its temple is the Lord God the Almighty and the Lamb ... the glory of God is its light and its lamp is the Lamb'.

As Thomas Aquinas wrote, 'types and shadows have their ending'. What can only be hinted at here in this life, will be made clearly manifest in the life of the world to come. Even the Eucharist itself, the mainstay of the Christian life in this world, will be caught up and transcended in the great messianic banquet of heaven, the marriage feast of the Lamb (Revelation 19.1–10).

In a famous phrase, the catechism answers the question of what is the whole purpose and destiny of humankind by saying that it is to know God and to enjoy the divine reality for ever. That is the most exciting prospect that there could possibly be, for it asserts that the fullness of joy and love, of truth and acceptance, things that we all long for in our heart of hearts, will indeed be given us in the life of heaven. This is a gift for whose reception finite and sinful human beings need to be prepared. We cannot just burst into the divine presence after death. Hence the need for judgement and purgation that we considered in the week of Advent 2.

Tomorrow we shall try to think a little more about what this heavenly sacramental life might be like. Meanwhile, we can open our hearts to hear and receive again the invitation that is extended to us, through the mercy of God, to enter into the salvation that leads to unending life in the divine presence:

> The Spirit and the bride say, 'Come.'
> And let everyone who hears say, 'Come.'
> And let everyone who is thirsty come.
> Let anyone who wishes take the water of life as a gift.
>
> (Revelation 22.17)

The Eucharist is the foretaste of the wholly sacramental life that awaits the believer in heaven. Let us thank God for that great anticipatory gift.

Prayer

> Therefore we, before him bending,
>   this great sacrament revere:
> types and shadows have their ending,
>   for the newer rite is here;
> faith, our outward sense befriending,
>   makes our inward vision clear.
>
> (Thomas Aquinas)

Friday: The worship of Heaven

After this I looked, and there was a great multitude that no one could count, from every nation, from all tribes and peoples and languages, standing before the throne and before the Lamb, robed in white, with palm branches in their hands. They cried out in a loud voice, saying, 'Salvation belongs to our God who is seated on the throne, and to the Lamb!' And all the angels stood around the throne and around the elders and the four living creatures, and they fell on their faces before the throne and worshipped God, singing, 'Amen! Blessing and glory and wisdom and thanksgiving and honour and power and might be to our God for ever and ever! Amen.'

(Revelation 7.9–12)

To be truly human is to be embodied – hence the Christian hope is resurrection rather than simply spiritual survival. We are not apprentice angels. Similarly, I believe that it is intrinsic to being human that we are temporal beings, creatures of time and not destined to be the inhabitants of a timeless eternity. The new creation will surely have its own form of 'time', just as it will have its own form of 'matter'. There will be an everlastingly unfolding history in heaven.

Not everyone reacts enthusiastically to this idea of an everlasting world ahead of us. No doubt it would be nice to have a much longer life than is afforded us here – a few thousand years maybe. But *everlasting* life? Isn't there a danger that eventually we shall get bored? Even the greatest golf enthusiast might tire of the game after a thousand years of playing on an endless succession of different courses.

If we had to rely only on our own finite resources, these anxieties would be very much to the point. But, as we thought yesterday, the life of heaven will be lived in the clear presence of God's infinite reality. In the course of the unfolding 'time' of the new creation, we shall be drawn deeper and deeper into the unending exploration of the inexhaustible riches of the divine nature. Now that really is something to look forward to.

It is hard for us to grasp more than a tiny bit of what it all might mean. The proper answer to many of our queries about the life of heaven is to say, 'Wait and see'. Yet we may be sure that an important part of that everlasting encounter with God will be our participation in the worship of heaven. Here again there is a danger that inadequate imagery may make this seem a less than fully exciting prospect. It is certainly going to involve very much more than sitting on a cloud, strumming a harp and endlessly chanting Alleluias.

An antidote to that kind of foolish thinking is given us in the many passages in Revelation that present vivid and moving pictures of the worship of heaven. Today's verses are a good example. The great company of the redeemed is gathered before the throne of the Lamb, their Redeemer. A tremendous hymn of praise breaks forth, 'Amen! Blessing and glory and wisdom and thanksgiving and honour and power and might be to our God for ever and ever!' That long string of divine attributes conveys something of the inexhaustible glory and majesty of God's nature. Only the greatest music begins to give us an earthly glimpse of what that heavenly worship might be like – Handel's 'Hallelujah Chorus' or Bach's *Sanctus* from the Mass in B minor catch something of the celestial spirit.

It is not only the redeemed and the angelic host who participate in this worship. There are also the four living creatures (Revelation 4.6–8), symbolic figures who represent the presence of non-human creation in the heavenly chorus of praise. What that signifies about cosmic destiny is something that we still have to consider. Meanwhile we too can join in the heavenly chorus of praise.

Prayer

> You are worthy, our Lord and God,
>   to receive glory and honour and power,
> for you created all things,
>   and by your will they existed and were created.
> (Revelation 4.11)

Saturday: All creation

> *For the creation waits with eager longing for the revealing of the children of God; for the creation was subjected to futility, not of its own will but of the will of the one who subjected it, in hope that the creation itself will be set free from its bondage to decay and will obtain the freedom of the glory of the children of God.*
> (Romans 8.19–21)

Scientists who study the universe do not only peer into the past towards the Big Bang, but they also look forward into the future. I have to tell you that the long-term prospects are not encouraging. There are two possible scenarios, depending on whether cosmic expansion beats gravity, or gravity beats cosmic expansion. In the former case, the universe will continue to expand endlessly, getting progressively colder and more decayed as it does so. In the latter case, the universe will one day collapse back into a state of extreme heat and great density, so that what began with the Big Bang will end with the Big Crunch. These are predictions that we should take very seriously. It is either freeze or fry, as far as the universe's future is concerned. In other words, the cosmos will die just as surely as you and I will die, though it will take a great deal longer to do so, after many tens of billions of years rather than the tens of years that are our allotted span.

The fact of the matter is that the universe is condemned to eventual futility. We do indeed live in a world that is 'in bondage to decay'. What are the theologians to make of that? Their response to the prospect of cosmic death is really no different from their response to the prospect of human death. It is to point beyond these realities to the greater reality of God's everlasting faithfulness.

The whole of creation must matter to its creator, who will not abandon it to the forces of futility. Just as human beings have destinies beyond their deaths, so will all of creation have an appropriate destiny beyond its death. That destiny, of course, is for the old creation to be transformed into the new creation. Human hope and cosmic hope belong together. The 'matter' of the world to come, that we have been talking about up till now without sufficiently explaining where it might come from, will be the divinely transformed and redeemed matter of this decaying world. In fact, this has already begun to happen in the event of the empty tomb, for that tells us that Christ's risen and glorified body is the transformed form of his dead body. In Christ there is a destiny for matter as well as for humanity. Today's remarkable passage from Romans makes the same point: ultimately the whole creation is to 'obtain the freedom of the glory of the children of God'.

As always in these explorations of future hope, if we try to carry the issue a little further we find that it is difficult to be sure of understanding much of the detail of what this might involve. We can only speculate, relying on the firm conviction of God's faithfulness and trying to make use of such insight as we have into the character of the present creation. It seems to me that there will surely be animals in the life of the new creation, but perhaps not every animal that has ever lived (and I certainly hope, not every bacterium). Many people who value and respect animals nevertheless feel that it is permissible to cull a herd of deer that is short of food supply, humanely killing some individuals in order to preserve the animal community. If that is right, it seems to suggest that animals are to be valued rather more in their general type than in their separate individuality. There will be deer in the new creation, but not necessarily every deer that has ever been. Of course, in the case of pets, with their close association with humans, the evaluation is rather different, with much greater emphasis laid on particularity. Perhaps that will make their case different. I think we shall have to wait and see, but we may be sure that God cares for all creatures in the ways that are right and appropriate to their natures.

Prayer

> O Lord, how manifold are your works!
>   in wisdom you have made them all;
> the earth is full of your creatures …
> May the glory of the Lord endure for ever;
>   may the Lord rejoice in his works.
>
> (Psalm 104.24, 31)

Advent 4

The Blessed Virgin Mary

And he came to her and said, 'Greetings, favoured one! The Lord is with you' ... Then Mary said, 'Here am I, the servant of the Lord; let it be with me according to your word.'

(Luke 1.28, 38)

Apart from the well-known stories of the annunciation and the birth of Jesus, together with the visit to the temple when Jesus was 12 (Luke 2.41–51), there is not a lot in the New Testament about the mother of Jesus. Three of the Gospels tell us that when Jesus started his public ministry, drawing the crowds and attracting the hostile attention of the authorities, Mary and the rest of the family sought to be in touch, but he was not welcoming to them when they turned up to see him (Mark 3.31–35; also in Matthew 12 and Luke 8). They were worried and disturbed by the risks Jesus seemed to be taking and they wanted to persuade him to calm down and come home (Mark 3.21), something that he could not do once his public ministry had begun in response to God's call received at his baptism. Yet when Jesus hangs on the cross, John tells us that Mary was there, a watcher at his passion, and that Jesus committed her into the care of the beloved disciple (John 19.26–27). After that, we only hear of Mary once more. She is in Jerusalem after the ascension, a member of the little company that awaited the promised gift of the Holy Spirit (Acts 1.14). After that there is silence.

In the pages of the New Testament, Mary is nowhere near as prominent a figure as people like Peter, Paul or Barnabas. The contrast with the vast amount of attention and devotion

that she attracted later in the history of the Church, is very
striking. There are the icons and the statues, the elaborated
stories and doctrines, and the fact that the fifth-century
Council of Ephesus declared her to have the title *Theotokos*
(the one who gave birth to God). So, was all that later
Marian exuberance just an unfortunate form of excessive
exaggeration? Of course, there were dangers, particularly at
times when it seemed to have been forgotten that Mary rep-
resents for us the expression of the most profound form of
creaturely nature, but there would be very serious distortion
if she were accorded a status that seemed almost to verge on
the divine. The role of the Blessed Virgin is to sum up the
nature of the Church, rather than providing alternative and
easier access to the throne of grace. A true theology has
always known that this is so, but popular piety has not always
found it so easy to keep its feelings within proper bounds.

Having said all that, it would be an equally bad error not
to recognize that Mary must have been a most remarkable
woman, whom we should love and respect for the unique
role that she was called upon to play in God's great revelatory act of the incarnation. The angel says to her, 'Greetings,
favoured one! The Lord is with you.' God did not choose
Mary at random. There must have been a profound purity of
character that fitted her for the responsibility of being the
mother of Christ, for we know how very important the love
and influence of the mother is in the development of a
child. This does not mean that the home at Nazareth was
unreally free from any of the tensions of normal family life.
There was that incident in the temple when the young Jesus
stayed behind, giving his parents much anxiety when they at
last noticed that he was not with them in the returning pilgrim company. There were problems in Jesus' adult life, for
no human being – and Jesus was fully human in his relationships with his family – can escape from painful clashes of
duty, in his case the duty of respect for parents that is so central a value in Jewish life, and the duty of loyalty to God in
fulfilling the mission to which he had been called.

Mary's character is summed up in her obedient response

to the message of the angel. A prospect in many ways strange
and troubling had been set before her, but she recognized
that it represented God's will for her. The incarnation
required not only the divine initiative of the overshadowing
of the Holy Spirit, but also the willing acceptance of that
young peasant girl who spoke the tremendous words, 'Here
am I, the servant of the Lord; let it be with me according to
your word.' We must all feel profound gratitude for the faithful obedience of the Blessed Virgin Mary.

Prayer

Almighty God, who looked upon the lowliness of the Blessed
Virgin Mary and chose her to be the mother of your only
Son: grant that we who are redeemed by his blood may share
with her in the glory of your eternal kingdom; through Jesus
Christ your Son our Lord, who is alive and reigns with you in
the unity of the Holy Spirit, one God, now and for ever.

(Common Worship, 2000)

Monday: Hell

> *Then Death and Hades were thrown into the lake of fire. This is*
> *the second death, the lake of fire; and anyone whose name was not*
> *found written in the book of life was thrown into the lake of fire.*
> (Revelation 20.14–15)

Christians have sometimes rather wallowed in images of the
horrors of hell. There is Dante's *Inferno*, a long poem filled
with descriptions of the successive torture chambers of that
grim place. There are the weird and disturbing pictures of
Hieronymus Bosch, where foul demons munch on the bodies of the damned. There is the overheated rhetoric of generations of hell-fire preachers. And one has to admit, there
are also biblical passages like these two verses from
Revelation, with their account of the lake of fire and the second death. So is the God of love a sadist on the side? I do not
think so. Perhaps these verses are images of purgation, the
burning away of dross, rather than images of destruction, in

which a painful annihilation is imposed on those who have displeased God. Turning to the final Last Thing gives us the opportunity to rethink the issue of hell.

I do not believe that God's offer of mercy and salvation is only available to us in this life, for it stems from the unchanging nature of the divine love and that cannot alter. In saying that, I am not at all implying that our beliefs and actions here and now are not very important. If we deliberately turn away from God in this life, it will be all the more difficult and painful for us to turn back again later. But it will not be impossible, or ruled out by a God who says, 'You had your chance and missed it. Too bad, that's that!'

Yet I also do not believe that anyone will be carried kicking and screaming into the kingdom of heaven against their will. The offer of mercy is made, but it can be refused. Will there be those who will persist in that refusal without limit, resisting God for ever? I do not think that we can know the answer to that question, but if there are, they will be the inhabitants of hell. They are not there because they have been thrown away by an angry God who finally lost patience with them. The tragedy of hell is much worse than that, for they are there because they have chosen to be there. As the preachers say, the doors of hell are locked on the inside, its gates barred by its inhabitants to keep out the bright light of the saving divine presence.

In the nineteenth century, Christians began seriously to question what had been a traditional picture of hell as the place of infinite punishment for finite human sins. I think that questioning was a Spirit-inspired move, leading to a much needed correction of distorted theological thinking. I am glad that we no longer picture hell in the way that seemed so natural and unproblematic to Dante. Yet it would be a further theological mistake if we came to think that we did not need the concept of hell at all, as if the Four Last Things could simply be cut down to Three. To follow that line would be seriously to underestimate a challenge that we need to face: the fact of our need of God. When we thought about the Fall, we saw that its real meaning lay in human alienation from God and the mistaken belief that we can go it alone without need for the help of divine grace. Hell is the place where that mistake continues to be made for ever. It is the setting of an unremitting refusal to allow ourselves ever to attain to the fulfilment of the true humanity that God intends for us. We can only hope and pray that in the end no one will persist everlastingly in that defiance of God's mercy. If that is the case, then hell will be empty, and we may be sure that this would be in accord with God's good will for human destiny. It is open to us in this life to begin to take those Godward steps that will lead us away from the barrenness of hell.

Prayer

Grant us, Lord, the wisdom and the grace to use aright the time that is left to us here on earth. Lead us to repent of our sins, the evil we have done and the good we have not done; and strengthen us to follow in the steps of your Son, in the way that leads to the fullness of eternal life, through Jesus Christ our Lord.

(*Alternative Service Book*, 1980)

Tuesday: Grey, not red

What has come into being in him was life, and the life was the light of all people ... He came to what was his own, and his own people did not accept him.

(John 1.3b–4, 11)

This reading from John speaks of the Word who is the true source of light and life, and it goes on to tell of the refusal of that life by some to whom it was offered. The language is sober and restrained, but the reality that it describes is tragic indeed, for this rejection, if persisted in, is the choice of hell instead of heaven. We have seen that hell is the place where the divine life has deliberately been excluded.

Conventional pictures of hell have often portrayed it as a place of torment, of painful heat or (to use Dante's preferred image) deadly cold. Actually, I believe that its nature is different from what these symbols suggest, for if the light of life has been blocked out, hell must be a place of dreariness and utter desolation. It should not be painted red for torment, but grey for boredom.

The most convincing picture of hell that I know is given in C. S. Lewis' imaginative writing, *The Great Divorce*. For Lewis, hell is a grey and dreary town, so insignificant in its diminished reality that it is lost down a crack in the floor of heaven. Every so often, the inhabitants are offered a bus trip up to the heavenly realm to see if they would like to stay and live there permanently. When they arrive, they find the bright reality of heaven is painful for them to bear. The grass is so real that it cuts their feet. More seriously, in heaven they have to face the true nature of what their lives have been. The cost of reconciliation with someone against whom a life-long grudge has been cherished, is felt to be too hard a price to pay. The uncoiling of a life that has become curled in upon itself is a costly undertaking, even if liberty and life lie at the end of it. Sadly, most of the visitors prove unwilling to accept release into the life of heaven. At the end of the day, they get on the bus to return again to the subterranean greyness of hell.

Some people have felt that because the true life that comes from God has been excluded from hell, its inhabitants will become more and more wraith-like, eventually fading away into nothingness. Personally, I do not know what to think about this suggestion of eventual annihilation. It might seem a plausible scenario, but its completion would represent a final defeat for the love of God, and I cannot imagine that steadfast divine goodwill ever giving up totally on anyone. There are mysteries about future destiny that are beyond our abilities to resolve in this life. What we can do here is to resolve for ourselves not to be among those who turn away from the light, but rather to be with those who claim the promise expressed by John when he went on to write that 'to all who received him, who believed in his name, he gave power to become children of God, who were

born, not of blood or of the will of the flesh or the will of
man, but of God' (John 1.12–13).

Prayer
O God, whom the pure in heart alone can see, give us
integrity and singleness of heart, that we may truly seek you
and grow in your knowledge and love, through Jesus Christ
our Lord.

Wednesday: Holiness

> *But nothing unclean will enter it [he holy city], nor anyone who
> practises abomination or falsehood, but only those who are written
> in the Lamb's book of life.*

> (Revelation 21.27)

The picture of hell as a place of torment is something that I
feel I must reject, despite there being material in Revelation,
and even in the words of Jesus reported in the Gospels (such
as Matthew 10.28: 'Do not fear those who kill the body but
cannot kill the soul; rather fear him who can destroy both
soul and body in Gehenna [the place of burning]'), that
could be appealed to in support of such a view. Am I right to
do so, or am I just manipulating the testimony of scripture
to please my liberal-minded fancy? This is a serious question
that has to be faced. I want to say three things in response.

The first relates to how we use the Bible. I certainly want
to read it respectfully, and I believe that part of that respect
requires me to engage with it as a whole and not to try to
wrench isolated 'proof texts' out of the wider context of
scripture. The New Testament is dominated by the assurance
of the love of God made known in Christ. I cannot accept an
interpretation that does not fully acknowledge this fact. The
punitive verses that we are wrestling with now therefore have
to be understood in some way that does not do violence to
this central New Testament insight into steadfast divine love.
My other two points try to indicate the way in which this
might be possible.

The second point relates to the style of Jewish thinking and expression. Semitic writers and speakers favour boldness and starkness of speech. Not for them the carefully nuanced tones that are so congenial to Anglo-Saxon habits of thought. Jewish people express themselves in black and white, rather than in shades of grey. Thus, when a prophet wishes to represent God as expressing a preferential choice, he does so by having God say categorically, 'I have loved Jacob, but I have hated Esau' (Malachi 1.2–3). In interpreting the intensity of some of the punitive passages of scripture, we must take this stylistic inclination into account.

When this is done, one can accept the third point, which is the belief that the principal intent of these difficult passages is to underline the moral seriousness of life and conduct, rather than to give precise prescriptions of penalties that are to be inflicted for transgressions. We are back with the ideas that we thought about in the course of the week of Advent 2.

God is indeed holy, a God of moral purity who cannot compromise with unrighteousness. It is true of the holy city of the New Jerusalem that 'nothing unclean shall enter it, nor anyone who practises abomination or falsehood'. The dross of our lives will have to be purged away before we can enter its portals. But, as we have thought before, that will be a hopeful process of purification, rather than a destructive process of rejection. We need to pray that this process will already begin for us in this life.

Prayer

Almighty God, unto whom all hearts be open, all desires known, and from whom no secrets are hid: cleanse the thoughts of our hearts by the inspiration of thy Holy Spirit, that we may perfectly love thee, and worthily magnify thy holy name: through Christ our Lord.

(*Book of Common Prayer*, 1662)

Thursday: The sin against the Holy Spirit

'Truly I tell you, people will be forgiven for their sins and whatever blasphemies they utter; but whoever blasphemes against the Holy Spirit can never have forgiveness, but is guilty of an eternal sin' – for they had said, 'He has an unclean spirit.'

(Mark 3.28–30)

Today's subject is one that – at least in ages of greater scrupulousness than ours – caused much anguish to a number of spiritually sensitive souls. God is a forgiving God, but here Jesus speaks of a sin that can *never* be forgiven. How can I be sure that I have not committed this terrible sin and so am damned for ever?

The way to approach this problem is by taking note of the context in which the words of today's reading are reported. Jesus has been doing many remarkable works of healing. God is evidently at work in him, as can be recognized by anyone who is willing to let their eyes see what is happening. The authorities, however, are by no means inclined to this way of thinking. They do not want to recognize Jesus' God-given authority or to take his spiritual leadership seriously. Yet they cannot deny that he heals those in need who cross his path. So they think up a monstrous idea to explain it all away. The scribes claim that these remarkable events are not the work of God at all, but Jesus has gained these powers by being in league with Beelzebul, the prince of the powers of darkness. Jesus rightly ridicules the suggestion – how could being a collaborator with evil continually bring about these acts of goodness? It doesn't make sense, and the assertion only shows the desperation in unbelief of his opponents.

It is clear that Jesus is also saddened and disturbed by the remark of the scribes, for it reveals in them a stubborn refusal to allow truth to speak for itself and to be acknowledged. *This* is the sin against the Holy Spirit: deliberately calling white black, the absolute rejection of truth and the failure to recognize the presence of grace. It is unforgivable, not because of some arbitrary divine decree that this is so, but precisely because it puts the one who commits it in a position of total falsehood and of alienation from the God who is the only true source of forgiveness. It is like people who are lost in a dangerous wilderness but who refuse to trust the guide who has been sent out to rescue them and even go off in the opposite direction. Such people suffer the self-inflicted consequence of not allowing their need to be met. Forgiveness will not be imposed on anyone against their will. It has to be asked for and accepted. Those who treat Jesus as if he were an agent of the devil, have simply removed themselves from the possibility of receiving divine acceptance.

It has often been said, and rightly so, that those who worry about whether they have committed the sin against the Holy Spirit are exactly those who have not done so. Their very spiritual anxiety shows that they are seeking to be open to God's truth and to receive God's gift of forgiveness. It is part of the tragedy of those who fall into this sin, that they become so trapped in the unreality of their false position that they are unaware of the possibility that something has gone gravely wrong in their lives. Those who seek the truth will, as they respond to it, also receive forgiveness.

Prayer
Eternal God, who art the light of the minds that know thee, the joy of the hearts that love thee, and the strength of the wills that serve thee: Grant us so to know thee that we may truly love thee, and so to love thee that we may truly serve thee, whom to serve is perfect freedom, in Jesus Christ our Lord.

(St Augustine)

Friday: Cynicism

Pilate asked him, 'So you are a king?' Jesus answered, 'You say that I am a king. For this I was born, and for this I came into the world, to testify to the truth. Everyone who belongs to the truth listens to my voice.' Pilate asked him, 'What is truth?'

(John 18.37–38)

Pontius Pilate had a pretty thankless task as governor of Judea. This small frontier province of the Roman empire was a powder keg, liable to explode into serious trouble if its Jewish population felt that their religion, about which they were so sensitive, had been insulted in some way. Pilate had discovered this when he marched some of his troops into Jerusalem carrying their standards, which had on them an image of the emperor. Those touchy Jews had got upset by this act of 'idolatry', as they saw it, and they had made a big disturbance outside the governor's residence in Caesarea. Pilate had had to give way on that occasion, but sometimes one had to be firm, as he had been when he violently suppressed a protest about money, collected for the temple but being spent on the really useful project of an aqueduct. The governorship was a wearisome job for Pilate and one, moreover, that would lead nowhere in terms of career advancement.

Now Pilate was in Jerusalem again, come up from Caesarea as he did every year, to keep an eye on what was happening over the dangerous period of the Passover Festival, a time when the city was flooded with religiously roused Jews from all over the Mediterranean. This year there had been a lot of talk about a wandering prophet, Jesus of Nazareth, who had been drawing the crowds and raising the expectation in some people's minds that he might turn out to be the long-awaited Messiah. Now this man was before Pilate, brought there by the temple authorities, sensible cooperative Jews who could be relied upon to help the governor keep the province stable and free from serious disorder.

Pilate knew how one had to deal with trouble makers, but this man seemed different. The governor engaged him in conversation, which revealed that Jesus considered himself to be some kind of king, but 'not of this world'. Pilate was uneasy, for he could see that this was no ordinary rabble-rouser bent on whipping up the crowds into disorderly action. The conversation got serious and it turned to matters of truth. Then Pilate felt that this had gone far enough and he decided to draw back. After all, he was a practical man who knew that sometimes you have to be economical with the truth in order to preserve the stability of society. The governor wearily shrugged his shoulders and said, 'What is truth?' The conversation was at an end. Pilate would try to save Jesus from execution, but if the price proved to be too high, so that it could lead to trouble in the streets of Jerusalem, then he would have to be crucified. Pilate shared the view of Caiaphas, the high priest, that at the end of the day it is better that one man should die, even if innocent, than that the nation should be in trouble (John 11.50).

Pilate was not a man of overwhelming evil. That is what makes him such a disturbing figure. Pilate was an ordinary man, caught in an extraordinary situation and lacking the moral courage to do what is right rather than what seems politically expedient. His life was lived according to the maxim that in the 'real world' you cannot make an omelette without cracking eggs. This worldly cynicism is more corrupting than, at first sight, it might seem to be. It really is true that the road to hell is paved with good intentions, never carried out because they would have been too costly. It really is true that characters are degraded by dubious actions and shabby compromises and that expedient but immoral stratagems, undertaken in the hope that they will keep society in a reasonably quiet and manageable state, ultimately lead to the crucifixion of the truth.

Prayer

Lord, grant us persistence in our search for truth, integrity and righteousness in the decisions of our lives, and give us the guidance of your Holy Spirit.

Christmas

Christmas Eve: Mary or Augustus?

In those days a decree went out from Emperor Augustus that all the world should be registered ... While they were there, the time came for her to deliver her child. And she gave birth to her first-born son and wrapped him in bands of cloth, and laid him in a manger because there was no place for them in the inn.

(Luke 2.1, 6–7)

If you had been living in the Roman empire in the year in which Jesus was born, and someone had asked you who was the most important person then alive, the answer would have been absolutely obvious. Who else could it possibly be but the Roman emperor, Augustus? He was a truly remarkable man. Born the great-nephew of Julius Caesar, as a young man he had been involved in the civil wars and internecine struggles that for many years followed upon his great-uncle's assassination. Eventually Octavian (as he was then called) emerged victorious over all his rivals, and he was given the supreme power to rule by the Roman senate, assuming the title of Augustus. For 41 years he exercised his authority with great wisdom and skill, pacifying the empire and reforming its administration. Augustus is undoubtedly one of the great figures of antiquity. Hence the unhesitating answer to the question of who it was that really mattered at that time.

But that answer would have been wrong, for the most important person then alive was actually someone completely different. Incredible as it would have seemed, the true answer was a young woman living in a fringe province of the empire, just about to give birth to a child conceived in highly dubious circumstances. Mary, the mother of Jesus, was far more significant than the great emperor in Rome, sitting on his imperial throne, though no one knew that at the time. History looked at from God's perspective is quite different from history as the world judges it and awards its accolades.

Mary, of course, was on her way with her husband Joseph to the city of Bethlehem. About a thousand years earlier, Samuel had been sent by God to the same city to anoint one of the sons of Jesse to be king over Israel in place of Saul. It was natural to suppose that the son selected would be Eliab, Jesse's first-born. When the young man came before Samuel, he was strong and handsome and the man of God felt sure that here was the new king. But God thought otherwise and told Samuel that Eliab had not been chosen. 'Do not look on his appearance or on the height of his stature, because I have rejected him; for the Lord does not see as mortals see; they look on the outward appearance, but the Lord looks on the heart' (1 Samuel 16.7). Eventually it turned out that God's chosen one was David, the youngest son, someone of such slight apparent significance that he had been left looking after the flock and he was only called to appear before Samuel when the latter insisted that he must see all of Jesse's sons.

All the time there are two quite different stories about what is happening. One is the public story, recorded in the newspapers and evaluated by public opinion. The other is the secret spiritual story, largely veiled from public view, a hidden leaven at work within society. One is the history of people like Augustus, whose empire was a great achievement, though one that lasted only a few hundred years. The other is the history of people like Mary, the history of the kingdom of God, that will continue for ever.

Prayer

Heavenly Father, who chose the Blessed Virgin Mary to be the mother of the promised saviour, fill us your servants with your grace, that in all things we may embrace your holy will and with her rejoice in your salvation; through Jesus Christ our Lord.

(*Common Worship*, 2000)

Christmas Day: The Word made flesh

And the Word became flesh and lived among us, and we have seen his glory, the glory as of a father's only son, full of grace and truth … From his fullness we have all received, grace upon grace. The law indeed was given through Moses; grace and truth came through Jesus Christ. No one has ever seen God. It is God the only Son, who is close to the Father's heart, who has made him known.
(John 1.14, 16–18)

At the heart of Christianity there is a most exciting idea: that the invisible God, mysterious in the infinity of the divine nature and beyond any finite human power to grasp, the One whom Moses could only approach in the clouds and thick darkness of Sinai, has acted to make God's character known in the clearest and most accessible way possible for us, by living the life of a human being in Jesus Christ. This is what Christmas is really about: the Word made flesh; the divine made known in human terms. 'No one has ever seen God. It is God the only Son, who is close to the Father's heart, who has made him known.'

Of course it is not at all easy to understand how this could be true, how the infinite could be focused onto the finite life of a human being, however remarkable that person might be. It was the last sort of idea which would have occurred naturally to the writers of the New Testament. They were almost all Jews and it is central to the Jewish faith to proclaim, 'Hear O Israel: the Lord is one God, the Lord alone' (Deuteronomy 6.4). God is One and will not share the divine glory with any other being. To God alone belongs the title 'Lord', used by pious Jews as a reverent way of referring to the One whose name was too holy ever to be uttered aloud. Yet in the New Testament we repeatedly find this title being assigned also to Christ, in the words of a second great proclamation, 'Jesus is Lord' (Romans 10.9; 1 Corinthians 12.3; etc.). Those monotheistic Jews who were followers of Jesus, felt that they had to make both of these proclamations of lordship, for they had found that they could not adequately speak of their experience of the risen Christ without being driven to use divine language about him. A scientist (particularly one who has worked in quantum physics) knows that sometimes the sheer weight of the evidence will force one to conclusions that, in terms of prior expectation, seem totally strange and paradoxical. When this happens, the only way to make progress is to hold on to the experience, even if one does not fully see how to make sense of it.

The doctrine of the incarnation, the idea of the Word made flesh, did not arise out of ungrounded speculation but out of the undeniable character of the encounter of the first disciples with the post-Easter Christ. It took the Church centuries of theological struggle to sort out how it ought to express its belief about these matters. In the end, the Church concluded that the only way to do so, which was faithful to its experience, was to believe that in Jesus Christ there is the union of two natures, one human, one divine.

Later in John's Gospel, Philip says to Jesus, 'Lord, show us the Father, and we shall be satisfied' (John 14.8). He speaks for all humanity in articulating the deep desire to know the nature of ultimate reality, to learn what the invisible God is really like. Jesus' reply is very simple and direct: 'Have I been with you all this time Philip, and you still do not know me? Whoever has seen me has seen the Father' (v. 9). Do you wonder if God, the Ruler of this vast universe, really loves and cares for individual human beings on planet earth, who are inhabitants of what is just a speck of cosmic dust floating among the trillions of stars that surround us? Look at Jesus and see if he cared for those in need who crossed his path. He certainly did, and so we may be sure that his heavenly Father does so also.

One of the greatest thinkers of Roman antiquity was St Augustine. He had pursued a long philosophical search for truth before finally he became a Christian. He tells us that when he read the prologue to John's Gospel, he found much that was already familiar to his Platonic way of thinking, until he came to verse 14. In the idea of the Word made *flesh*, Augustine found something entirely new. He learned that the great Platonic ideals of truth and beauty and goodness were not only abstract values forming the everlasting basis of reality, but they had also come down to earth to be fully displayed, embodied in the life and death and resurrection of Jesus Christ. Christmas is the time when we mark and celebrate the beginning of the great revelatory act of the incarnation, a time when we can truly rejoice that it has been given to us to see 'his glory, the glory as of a father's only son, full of grace and truth'.

Prayer

Christ is born, give glory. Christ comes from heaven, meet him. Christ is on earth, be exalted. O all the earth, sing unto the Lord, and sing praises in gladness, O all you people, for he has been glorified.

(Eastern Liturgy)

St Stephen: Following Christ

But they covered their ears, and with a loud shout all rushed together against him. Then they dragged him out of the city and began to stone him; and the witnesses laid their coats at the feet of a young man named Saul. While they were stoning Stephen, he prayed, 'Lord Jesus, receive my spirit.' Then he knelt down and cried out in a loud voice, 'Lord do not hold this sin against them.' When he had said this, he died.

(Acts 7.57–60)

For most of us the Feast of Stephen has been turned into Boxing Day, the opportunity, perhaps, for a brisk country walk to dispel the effects of overindulgence on the preceding day. We have lost something by this change.

Stephen was a rather radical young man, one of the recently appointed deacons whose job it was to look after the needy members in the young church in Jerusalem. He had grasped very clearly that the coming of Christ implied changes in people's understanding of how God was to be worshipped and served, and this had made him enemies among more conservative-minded temple worshippers. A group of them had banded together to set Stephen up on a trumped-up charge of blasphemy. There was a lot of anger around and Stephen's vigorous defence before the authorities, based on an account of Israel's history that emphasized the nation's rebellious tendencies in the past, did nothing to calm the situation. He burst out, 'You stiff-necked people, uncircumcised in heart and ears, you are for ever opposing the Holy Spirit, just as your ancestors used to do' (Acts 7.51). The reaction was instant and intense. Stephen was dragged outside the city to become the first Christian martyr, stoned to death by an angry mob.

The way that Acts tells this violent story is intended to bring out the parallels between this death and the death of Jesus, Stephen's Master. Both are unjustly condemned by a hostile meeting of the religious leaders. At his death, Stephen commits his spirit to the Lord, just as Jesus had committed his spirit into the hands of his heavenly Father (Luke 23.46). Stephen prays that the sin of his lynching will not be held against his persecutors, just as Jesus had asked for forgiveness for those who were crucifying him (Luke 23.34). Just before his death Stephen had been given a vision of the risen and exalted Christ: '"Look", he said, "I see the heavens opened and the Son of Man standing at the right hand of God!"' (Acts 7.56).

Christians are called to follow in the footsteps of Christ. Jesus spoke stern words to his disciples about this, 'If any want to become my followers, let them deny themselves and take up their cross daily and follow me' (Luke 9.23). For Stephen, and for some Christians in every century since, including this one, that has meant faithfulness even unto the death of martyrdom. Jesus warned his followers, 'If they persecuted me, they will persecute you' (John 15.20).

For most of us, of course, our Christian commitment may

bring us no more than the occasional snide remark or pity-
ing smile. Yet it is good for all of us to remember the Feast
of Stephen. It reminds us of the seriousness of our disciple-
ship, and it encourages us to pray for our brothers and sisters who even now are facing hardship, and even possible
death, for the faith of Christ.

Prayer
Uphold, O God, all those who are persecuted or imprisoned
for their beliefs. Be to them a light showing the way ahead;
a rock giving them strength to stand; a song singing of all
things overcome.

(Bishop Richard Harries)

St John the Evangelist: Simple words – profound truth

> *Now Jesus did many other signs in the presence of his disciples,
> which are not written in this book. But these things are written so
> that you may come to believe that Jesus is the Messiah, the Son of
> God, and that through believing you may have life in his name.*
> (John 20.30–31)

St John's Gospel is one of the most profound books ever written. Its spiritual power is immense, and it has sustained and
inspired countless people in their Christian pilgrimage. Even
to the most casual reader, it is apparent that this Gospel is written in a different style from that of the other three. In
Matthew, Mark and Luke, the way in which Jesus talks is by way
of pithy sayings and vivid parables, rooted in the everyday life
of first-century Palestine. In John, Christ talks in tones that
have something of the nature of eternity about them. In place
of the parables we have a sequence of great symbolic repre-
sentations of the significance of the Word made flesh: the
Bread from Heaven, the Good Shepherd, the True Vine. Early
in the Church's history, this special character of John was
clearly recognized and it was seen as being a 'spiritual Gospel'

in a very special sense. Tradition suggests that the book origi-
nated in the reflections in old age of that disciple who had
been specially close to Jesus and who, just before his death,
shared the fruits of his life-long meditation on the life, death
and resurrection of the one whom he had known so well. The
Gospel conveys Christian truth in its deepest possible form.

This spiritual character of John by no means implies that
its author was not also concerned with matters of historical
truth. We are told that these things were written to record
the signs that Jesus did in the presence of his disciples. A
close reading of all four Gospels will show that, in fact, there
is more geographical and chronological detail in John than
there is in the other three. The evangelist is not simply concerned with timeless truths but also with 'what we have
heard, what we have seen with our eyes, what we have looked
at and touched with our hands, concerning the word of life'
(1 John 1.1). To take an example, in chapter 5 there is a
story about the healing by Jesus of a man who had spent 38
years waiting for release from paralysis as he lay beside a
pool with curative waters 'called in Hebrew Beth-zatha,
which has five porticoes' (v. 2). Some older scholars, mind-
ful of John's spiritual concerns, suggested that maybe this
was a symbolic story, with the five porticoes standing for the
five books of Moses that make up the Jewish Torah. However,
archaeological excavations in Jerusalem have shown that
there was indeed such a pool and that it really did have five
porticoes. In John, as in all Christian thinking, there is a profound combination of the power of the eternally symbolic
with the power of the actually historically enacted.

It may come as something of a surprise to English readers
to learn that the Greek in which John is written is the simplest in the New Testament. Students learning New
Testament Greek start with John as their first text. The deepest theological insight is expressed in the simplest words. On
reflection, perhaps this is not so surprising after all. The
truth about Jesus is not some esoteric kind of secret that only
the most learned could hope to penetrate and understand.
The Gospel is the word of life, a life that is offered to every-

one, young or old, learned or unlearned. 'These things are written so that you may come to believe that Jesus is the Messiah, the Son of God, and that through believing you may have life in his name.'

Prayer
Merciful Lord, we beseech thee to cast thy bright beams of light upon thy Church, that it being enlightened by the doctrine of thy blessed Apostle and Evangelist Saint John may so walk in the light of thy truth that it may at length attain to the light of everlasting life; through Jesus Christ our Lord.

(*Book of Common Prayer*, 1662)

Holy Innocents: The bitterness of suffering

When Herod saw that he had been tricked by the wise men, he was infuriated, and he sent and killed all the children in and around Bethlehem who were two years old or under, according to the time that he had learned from the wise men.

(Matthew 2.16)

Three days after the joyous Feast of Christmas comes the sad remembrance of the holy innocents, the children slaughtered at the command of the ruthless King Herod as he sought to protect himself from any threat to the tenure of his throne. If Jesus had not been born, and if the magi had not called in at Jerusalem in the course of their search for him, naively enquiring where the new King of the Jews had been born, those children would have lived on into adult life. The adoration of the magi and the slaughter of the innocents are opposite sides of the same coin. Those mothers weeping in Bethlehem are the shadow side of the Christmas story.

Holy Innocents Day sets before us, with peculiar intensity and sharpness, the strange character of this present world, with its mixture of joy and sorrow, promise and pain. We are glad indeed that the Christ child was born, but why did it have to be at the cost of the deaths of his tiny contemporaries? Why did God not intervene to stop the massacre of the innocents? Come to that, why did God not intervene to stop Auschwitz? One of the saddest sights of that terrible place is a room where the Nazi guards piled up shoes taken from those who were about to enter the gas chambers. Thousands of pairs are stacked there, each one representing some person whose life was untimely destroyed. Many of those shoes are children's shoes.

Before the mystery of suffering we necessarily fall silent. We can understand that God has given humans free will and that this means that it can be, and it is, exercised in ways that are totally contrary to the divine purpose. But the bitterness of suffering is too great to be assuaged by logical arguments of this kind, true though they are in their own way. If there is to be a theological response to the problem of suffering, it has to lie much deeper than that. I believe that the Christian response does indeed lie very deep, for it speaks of a God who is not simply a compassionate spectator of the travail of creation but One who, in the cross of Christ, has actually participated in that suffering. God is truly a fellow sufferer with creation, for the Christian God is the crucified God. The life of the baby Jesus was saved by the flight into Egypt, but there was a cup waiting, prepared for him to drink, and when the time came, he drained it to the dregs.

Prayer

God of love, whose compassion never fails; we bring before thee the troubles and perils of peoples and nations, the sighing of prisoners and captives, the sorrows of the bereaved, the necessities of strangers, the helplessness of the weak, the despondency of the weary, the failing powers of the aged. O Lord, draw near to each; for the sake of Jesus Christ our Lord.

(St Anselm)

29 December: Divine vulnerability

Let the same mind be in you that was in Christ Jesus, who, though he was in the form of God, did not regard equality with God as something to be exploited, but emptied himself, taking the form of a slave, being born in human likeness. And being found in human form, he humbled himself and became obedient to the point of death – even death on a cross.

(Philippians 2.5–8)

If Jesus shows us what God is like, what do we learn about the divine character from the baby in the manger? I think that scene tells us something very surprising, namely that God is vulnerable, for what could be more vulnerable than a new-born baby? God is the all-powerful King of the universe, but God has chosen not to use that power in order to put a shield around the heavenly throne, in the way that Herod tried to put a shield around his throne to protect himself from the influence of others. The God who is the God of love could not act in that way, for love must always be open to being influenced by the beloved. In a word, the God of love must be vulnerable.

Two things need to be said about this. The first is that this vulnerability is not imposed on God from the outside, but it is freely chosen from within, according to the dictates of love. That choice involves a divine self-limitation, or 'kenosis' as the theologians say. The word comes from the Greek of the verses from Philippians. The passage tells us that Christ did not cling on to equality with God but emptied himself (the Greek is *ekenosen*), becoming human, even to the point of human death – in fact, to the point of the painful and shameful death of crucifixion. The baby in the manger, and the man hanging on the gallows of the cross, are images enacted within time of God's self-emptying love that is eternally part of the divine nature. Here we see again from a slightly different perspective, the truth we encountered yesterday, that God is not an invulnerable being high above the painful process of the world, but One who understands suffering from the inside and who fully shares in the travail of creation.

The second thing that must be said is that though God accepts vulnerability, God does not give up and accept defeat. God is ceaselessly at work to bring about fulfilment and salvation, even if this is brought about by the patient process of love, rather than by a naked exercise of over-whelming power. The story of Jesus did not end with the crucifixion but it continued through to the resurrection. Our passage from Philippians about Christ's self-emptying humility is immediately followed by a passage about Christ's exaltation. 'Therefore God also highly exalted him and gave him the name that is above every name ... [that] every tongue should confess that Jesus Christ is Lord, to the glory of God the Father' (Philippians 2.9, 11).

Prayer

Almighty God, Father of our Lord Jesus Christ, who hast sent thy Son to take our nature, and hast made him to become the Son of man, that we might become the sons and daughters of God: Grant that we, being conformed to his humility and sufferings, may be partakers of his resurrection; through the same Jesus Christ our Lord.

(after Jeremy Taylor)

30 December: Faithful Joseph

Now the birth of Jesus the Messiah took place in this way. When his mother Mary had been engaged to Joseph, but before they lived together, she was found to be with child from the Holy Spirit. Her husband Joseph, being a righteous man and unwilling to expose her to public disgrace, planned to dismiss her quietly.

(Matthew 1.18–19)

The scene in the stable after the birth of Jesus is one we have seen portrayed in a hundred paintings and on countless Christmas cards. A light shines on the central figures of the young mother and the baby. Also in the foreground there may be some awestruck shepherds, or three gorgeously clad kings offering their gifts. The background is dark, but one can just make out some shadowy figures. Two of them are animals, an ox and an ass. And there is also an elderly man just visible in the shadows. He is Joseph, the unsung hero of the Christmas story. He deserves our closer attention.

Joseph had been engaged to Mary, a young woman of evident piety. It must have been a dreadful shock to him to discover that she was pregnant before their marriage. Joseph did not know who the father might be, but his generous nature inclined him not to make a public scandal of Mary, but to bring their engagement quietly to an end. Then Joseph learned the almost incredible news that the coming child is 'from the Holy Spirit' and destined to play a unique role in God's salvific plans. Joseph was able to trust that this is really so, though he must have been only too aware that the neighbours would not see it this way and that they would treat him as someone who had been badly deceived. Joseph stood by Mary and her expected child, and he cared for them as they trudged the weary way to Bethlehem. After the birth there comes another disturbing message. Herod is seeking the child to take his life. Instantly and decisively, Joseph acts, hastening the family to safety in Egypt.

How different the Christmas story would have been without the rock-solid faithfulness of Joseph! We often take him for granted, but his role was indispensable. Joseph stands as an example of utter reliability and trustworthiness in strange and disturbing circumstances, able to act with generosity and effectiveness. Matthew makes it clear that God communicated with Joseph principally through significant dreams. This makes him unique among New Testament characters, reminding us that God often deals with different people in different ways. God may speak to us in some totally different fashion, but we should all pray that we may be given grace to follow the example of the trusting response of God's faithful servant, Joseph.

Prayer

Almighty God, who called Joseph to be the husband of the Virgin Mary, and the guardian of your only Son, open our eyes and our ears to the messages of your holy will, and give us courage to act upon them; through Jesus Christ our Lord.

(Alternative Service Book, 1980)

31 December: The pilgrim path

Therefore, since we are surrounded with so great a cloud of witnesses, let us also lay aside every weight and the sin that clings so closely, and let us run with perseverance the race that is set before us, looking to Jesus the pioneer and perfecter of our faith, who for the sake of the joy that was set before him endured the cross, disregarding its shame, and has taken his seat at the right hand of the throne of God.

(Hebrews 12.1–2)

Another year comes to an end. We have lived through a further year of life, and we are one year nearer our death. All the Abrahamic faiths (for Judaism, Christianity and Islam all agree about this) see life as a pilgrim path being trodden in the course of a journey of worship and obedience that is taking us towards our spiritual destiny. The unknown person who wrote the letter to the Hebrews uses the image of a race in which we are all running towards the finishing line of salvation in the presence of God. We are given four important thoughts about this pilgrim's progress.

The first is that it calls for perseverance. The spiritual race is a long-distance event, not a short sprint. Jesus had expressed a similar thought in the course of his parable of the sower. The seed that fell on rocky ground soon shot up, but it had no root and quickly withered away because it could not endure the heat of the sun (Mark 4.16–17). Bearing fruit takes time. It is not the start that really counts, but the ability to carry right on to the end.

The second thought is that running requires the athlete to be stripped down for action, concentrating on the goal ahead and not burdened with superfluous baggage. Our spiritual race requires that we set aside 'the sin that clings so closely'.

The third thought is that the race is not a solo perform-
ance. The path on which we are running is already well-trod-
den, for many have gone before us, and as we run we are in
the company of many others who are on their way to the
celestial city. It should be a big encouragement that we are
'surrounded by so great a cloud of witnesses'.

Finally, the fourth thought is that all these spiritual ath-
letes are in the hands of a supremely experienced and mas-
terly Trainer. We run the race of our pilgrimage 'looking to
Jesus the pioneer and perfecter of our faith, who for the
sake of the joy that was set before him endured the cross, disregarding its shame'. We shall not be asked to go where he
has not been before.

May his presence be with us as we begin this new year, the
next lap of our spiritual journey.

Prayer

O Lord Christ, who art both Alpha and Omega, the beginning and the end, and whose years shall not fail: Grant us so
to pass through the coming year with faithful hearts, that in
all things we may please thee and glorify thy name; who livest
and reignest with the Father and the Holy Ghost, ever one
God, world without end.

(Ancient Mozarabic Sacramentary)

Epiphany

Naming of Jesus: Saviour

She will bear a son, and you are to name him Jesus, for he will save his people from their sins.

(Matthew 1.21)

Eight days after his birth, in accordance with the prescription of the Jewish law, Mary's son was circumcised and given his name. The angel had instructed Joseph what that name should be. We call him Jesus, the Greek version of a Hebrew name that was, in fact, quite a common one, being the same as Joshua, the leader who had succeeded Moses and led Israel out of the wilderness into the promised land. Its meaning is 'The Lord is salvation'.

Names were very important in the ancient world, for they were believed to be closely aligned to the nature of the person to whom they had been given. The name bestowed on that baby was no random choice, for it foreshadowed what God intended the significance of his life to be. Jesus is the saviour.

The dream message of the angel had also made it clear what kind of deliverance it would be that Jesus was to bring. He is to 'save his people from their sins'. We have already thought of the human plight, our alienation from the God who is the only true source of life and fulfilment for humanity. Jesus came to end that state of affairs, to provide the salvific bridge by which we might find our way back into a sharing of the life and energies of God that is our true destiny. This is what theologians sometimes call 'the work of Christ', the achievement of his life and of his death.

Jesus did not do this work simply by offering us good advice (as in the Sermon on the Mount), or even by showing us how this advice was actually followed and lived out in his own life. Advice and example are not enough for humanity. We need help. That exemplary life is wonderful and inspiring to behold and to meditate upon, but how could it actually work for us, in our lives? We can listen to the command to love our enemies (Matthew 5.44), and we can certainly see that Jesus did just this when we read of him asking for forgiveness for those who were nailing him to the cross (Luke 23.34), but how are we to live that kind of life ourselves? Anger and resentment so quickly creep in. There is a weight of sin that distorts our lives and frustrates our good resolutions. We need more than advice and example; we need salvation, a power that will save us from our sinful selves.

It has been the consistent experience and witness of the Christian Church throughout the centuries that this power does come to those who trust in Jesus as their saviour. He was sent by the Father through the overshadowing of the Holy Spirit, so that he could live a truly human life and accept a truly human death. In this way the life of God and the life of humanity were joined together in a manner that did not only work for Jesus himself, but which can also overflow from him into the lives of those who look to him for salvation. Theologians have discussed for many centuries how it might be possible to understand the effectiveness of this work of Christ. So-called theories of the atonement (the at-one-ment of divine and human life) have been devised, but none has received the total and final endorsement of the Christian Church. They offer us important insights, but it seems that the mystery of salvation is too deep for exhaustive explanation.

This lack of understanding does not at all alter the *fact* of that saving experience. We do not need to possess a correct theological explanation before we can enter into salvific experience. Any physicist knows that it is possible to encounter strange and unexpected phenomena that are very hard to understand (light is waves/light is particles), but we do not make any progress in physics by denying that experience just because we do not yet have a theory about it. It is the same in the life of the Church. Generations of Christians have come to know Jesus as the One who delivers his people from their sins. That is enough for us to be able to confess him as our saviour.

Prayer

O saviour of the world, who as on this day wast called Jesus, according to the word of the angel: Fulfil unto us, we beseech thee, the gracious promise of that holy name, and, of thy great mercy, save thy people from their sins; who, with the Father and the Holy Ghost, livest and reignest one God world without end.

(Irish Prayer Book)

2 January: Prophet

> *And he rolled up the scroll, gave it back to the attendant, and sat down. The eyes of all in the synagogue were fixed on him. Then he began to say to them, 'Today this scripture has been fulfilled in your hearing.' All spoke well of him and were amazed at the gracious words that came from his mouth.*

(Luke 4.20–22a)

In the history of Israel we can distinguish a number of different vocations through which people might be called to the service of God. Among the most important of these were the categories of prophet, priest and king. Reformation theologians, such as John Calvin, liked to think about the nature and work of Christ by affirming that in him all these three roles were simultaneously fulfilled. In the next three days we shall focus our thoughts on Jesus by considering these three offices in turn. Today we think of Jesus as prophet.

It is a preacher's cliché to say that prophets are concerned with 'forthtelling' rather than 'foretelling'. They are not fortune tellers, helpfully furnished with a divinely guaranteed crystal ball in which they can perceive the details of future events, but they are those who are guided by God's Spirit to discern something of the movement of history that is hidden from the perceptions of more ordinary people. The role of the prophet is to speak 'the word of the Lord' to the contemporary situation, in warning and exhortation.

In today's passage, Jesus is in his home synagogue and he has just read the powerful words of an earlier prophet, Isaiah, that affirm that there will be 'a year of the Lord's favour', in which the poor and oppressed will receive good news and experience deliverance (Luke 4.16–19). Jesus tells his hearers that these words are now coming to pass and that they find their fulfilment in his own words and deeds. At first the congregation are favourably impressed, but later, when he speaks about the particularity of God's actions and how hard it is for a prophet to be accepted in his home town, they become offended and even try to do him serious physical harm (Luke 4.23–30). The vocation of a prophet has always been a difficult and dangerous one. Often the words that have to be spoken are painful and unpalatable to their hearers. No wonder that Jeremiah was reluctant to accept his own calling (Jeremiah 1.5–6; 20.7–18).

Later in Luke, Jesus prophesies concerning his own destiny, three times speaking of his coming suffering and subsequent vindication (Luke 9.21–22, 43–45; 18.31–34). The terms in which these utterances are expressed are rather general. I think that we may be sure that Jesus' prophetic insight enabled him to realize that in Jerusalem he would face his final confrontation with the authorities and that they would impose their worldly power upon him by condemning him to death. I am equally sure that he trusted that his heavenly Father would eventually vindicate his cause. Yet I do not at all believe that Jesus saw the events of Holy Week laid out before him in a detailed preview. That would have meant that Gethsemane would have been a kind of charade, which is an impossible thought about what is one of the most profoundly moving and significant episodes in the whole gospel story.

The essential role of the prophet is the fearless utterance of truth. Jesus did not only fulfil that role, but he was himself the Truth that was to be proclaimed (John 14.6). In him the message and the messenger coincided.

Prayer

O Lord almighty, Father of Jesus Christ our Lord, grant us, we pray thee, to be grounded and settled in thy truth by the coming down of thy Holy Spirit in our hearts. That which we know not do thou reveal; that which is wanting in us, do thou fill up; that which we know do thou confirm, and keep us blameless in thy service; through the same Jesus Christ our Lord.

(St Clement of Rome, first century)

3 January: Priest

Since, then, we have a great high priest who has passed through the heavens, Jesus, the Son of God, let us hold fast to our confession. For we do not have a high priest who is unable to sympathize with our weaknesses, but we have one who in every respect has been tested as we are, yet without sin. Let us therefore approach the throne of grace with boldness, so that we may receive mercy and find grace to help in time of need.

(Hebrews 4.14–16)

In ancient Israel, the priest stood between God and the people. On the one hand, he represented the humanity of the assembled worshippers, while, on the other hand, he was given privileged access on their behalf to the divine presence, offering sacrifices of thanksgiving and worship, as well as sacrifices of atonement for the sins of the nation. Once a year only, the high priest was allowed to enter the holy of holies, the inner and most sacred space in the temple, and to utter the divine name that on all other occasions it would have been blasphemy to speak aloud. For the rest of the year, the ordinary sacrificial cult of temple worship was faithfully maintained, day by day. The priesthood itself, of course, had periodically to be renewed as younger members of the house of Aaron replaced their elders who had died.

The letter to the Hebrews is a sustained meditation on how these rites of the old covenant were foreshadowings of the eternal rite of the new covenant, exercised by the exalted Christ before the throne of grace in the realm of heaven. Jesus 'holds his priesthood permanently, because he continues for ever. Consequently he is able for all time to save those who approach God through him, since he always lives to make intercession for them' (Hebrews 7.24–25).

This everlasting ministry of intercessory prayer is a unique aspect of Christ's priestly ministry. Another contrast with the character of earthly priesthood lies in the fact that Christ is not only the one who offers sacrifice, as the priests in the temple presented their daily round of animal sacrifices, but – through his death on the cross – he is himself the sacrifice that is offered. 'But when Christ came as a high priest of the good things that have come … he entered once for all into the Holy Place, not with the blood of goats and calves, but with his own blood, thus obtaining eternal redemption' (Hebrews 9.11–12).

The concept of sacrifice is not at all an easy one for us today. If God wants to forgive us, why doesn't that just happen, without any further fuss about it? I have to confess that I have to struggle here to try to gain some insight. At least, we can recognize from our own experience that true forgiveness is not a trivial matter, but it is a very costly process. It is very far from saying, 'That's all right. It doesn't really matter. Forget it!' We can see this costliness of forgiveness clearly enough in human life. A couple whose child has been killed by a drunken motorist may have the great generosity to forgive that crime, but it must be a very painful and difficult matter for them to do so. In some analogous way, God's forgiveness is not painless either. In some way, the death of the Son of God on the cross is the expression in history of the eternal costliness of the eternal act of divine forgiveness.

The final thing to say about the priesthood of Christ

relates to the theme of the solidarity of the priest with those on whose behalf he pleads. Jesus was without sin, but he was not in the least without experience of temptation and times of trial. As Jesus intercedes for us in heaven, he does so as one through whom we may 'approach the throne of grace with boldness, so that we may receive mercy and find grace to help in time of need'.

Prayer

O God, whose blessed Son, our great High Priest, has entered once for all into the holy place, and ever liveth to intercede on our behalf: Grant that we, sanctified by the offering of his body, may draw near with full assurance of faith by the way that he has dedicated for us, and evermore serve thee, the living God; through the same thy Son our Lord Jesus Christ, who liveth and reigneth with thee, O Father, and the Holy Spirit, one God, world without end.

(Church of South India)

4 January: King

God put this power to work in Christ when he raised him from the dead and seated him at his right hand in the heavenly places, far above all rule and authority and power and dominion, and above every name that is named, not only in this age but also in the age to come.

(Ephesians 1.20–21)

My college in Cambridge held an annual feast on Ascension Day. One year, I invited a visiting colleague to come with me to this dinner as my guest. She came from a very secular background in the United States and she was intrigued that an academic institution should hold a special celebration on a religious festival. As we talked about it, I realized with some unease that Loretta was confusing Ascension with Easter. Of course, I had to explain that it was something different, 'When – you know – he went up into heaven.' It did not go down well. I was embarrassed because I could see that my friend had in her mind a picture of Jesus setting out on some kind of space journey. 'What a weirdo belief', she must have been thinking.

It was only later that I came to realize what I should have said to Loretta. I ought to have told her that Ascension Day is the Feast of Christ the King. The spatial imagery in the story is about exaltation and not about moving off through the solar system. The true meaning of the ascension is very well expressed in these two verses from Ephesians.

When we think about Jesus' office as king, we are engaging with the question of what is going on in the history of the world. We see a very mixed scene as we look around us, a world of promise and of frustration, with both intuitions of hope and also experiences of evil and tyranny. It seems a perplexing mixture of light and darkness. Will the battle between them continue for ever, ebbing and flowing as it seems to have done for so many centuries already? Is anyone really in charge of what is happening? Will there be an eventual victory of good over evil?

The kingship of Christ asserts a positive answer to these questions. While it is true, as the writer to the Hebrews wryly observes, 'As it is, we do not yet see everything in subjection to [God]', yet it is also true that 'we do see Jesus, who for a little while was made lower than the angels, now crowned with glory and honour' (Hebrews 2.8–9). He is the shape of the future. His is the will that finally shall prevail. At present, Christ's kingship is veiled, but the time will come when it will be fully revealed. The truth of the matter is that, in the ultimate purposes of God, he is 'far above all rule and authority and power and dominion, and above every name that is named, not only in this age but also in the age to come'.

Prayer

Almighty and everlasting God, who hast willed to restore all things in thy well-beloved Son, the King and Lord of all: Mercifully grant that all peoples and nations, divided and wounded by sin, may be brought under the gentle yoke of

his most loving rule; who with thee and the Holy Spirit liveth
and reigneth, ever one God, world without end.

(Sarum Breviary)

5 January: Jesus is Lord

*To all God's beloved in Rome, who are called to be saints: Grace
to you and peace from God our Father and the Lord Jesus Christ.*

(Romans 1.7)

As far as we can make out, the earliest of all Christian con-
fessions seems to have been 'Jesus is Lord'. This first
Christian creed is very short, but it is a more profound and
startling statement than at first it might appear to be.

In everyday speech in the ancient Greek-speaking world,
people would use 'lord' simply as a respectful form of
address, rather like the English use of 'sir', which does not
carry the implication that the person addressed is actually a
knight. But 'Lord' used as a title was something entirely different. We have seen already that Jews used this as one of
their words for God, thereby avoiding uttering the divine
name that was too holy ever to be uttered aloud by ordinary
people. To say that 'Jesus is Lord' is a very odd thing for a
Jew to do.

In today's single verse we see St Paul, a deeply Jewish person if there ever was one (2 Corinthians 11.22), opening his
letter to the Romans with the customary greeting that he
used at the start of most of his correspondence: 'Grace to
you and peace from God our Father and the Lord Jesus
Christ'. When we read Paul we tend to skip over these preliminary formalities and get on to whatever that particular
letter is mainly about. In fact, it is well worth stopping to ask
ourselves what is going on in these words of greeting. When
we look closely at them we see something quite startling.
Paul is bracketing together God and Jesus, as if there is some
sort of deep connection, even similarity, between the
Almighty and Invisible God of Israel, whose name even is too
holy to be spoken aloud, and this Jewish man who was alive

only a little while ago. You could not imagine any Jew put-
ting God and Moses together in this way, remarkable man
though Moses undoubtedly was. When those early Christians
confessed that 'Jesus is Lord', they were affirming that there
was something utterly unique about him, so that he alone of
all people who have ever lived could properly be spoken of
in this way, using not only obvious human language but also
very far from obvious divine-sounding language as well.

That is as far as the New Testament takes the matter. It
very seldom says straight out that Jesus is divine (John 20.28
is perhaps the clearest example), but all the time it is assign-
ing to him the kind of lordship that can only really belong
to God. It took centuries of spiritual and intellectual struggle for the Church to work out how it ought to think about
the implications of these astonishing insights. In the end,
the only understanding that proved adequate to the continuing experience of the lordship of the risen and exalted
Christ was the incarnational and trinitarian belief that Jesus
was the divine Word made human flesh, so that in him there
was indeed found both human nature and divine nature. We
have already thought that in this conviction is to be found
the very core of the Christian faith. Endless learned books of
theology have been written exploring this great mystery, but
it can be grasped by the simplest believers as they confess
'Jesus is Lord'.

Prayer

O Lord Jesus Christ, who hast said that thou art the way, the
truth and the life: suffer us not at any time to stray from
thee, who art the way; nor to distrust thy promises, who art
the truth; nor to rest in any other than thee, who art the life;
beyond which there is nothing to be desired, neither in
heaven, nor in earth; for thy Name's sake.

(Erasmus)

Epiphany: Gentiles and intellectuals

In the time of King Herod, after Jesus was born … wise men from
the East came to Jerusalem, asking, 'Where is the child who has
been born king of the Jews? For we observed his star at its rising,
and have come to pay him homage.

(Matthew 2.1–2)

The first people from outside the family to see the baby Jesus
were some Jewish shepherds. Only later do the 'wise men
from the East', called in the Greek 'magi', arrive to pay their
homage. The term magus is rather a vague one, for it could
mean either a sage or a magician. Our translation opts for
the first alternative, and that certainly seems a plausible
choice to make. These visitors from the East probably came
from somewhere in the direction of Persia. A lot of what we
have come to believe we know about them really derives
from a long tradition in Christian art, itself mostly based on
legendary conjecture. The New Testament does not call
them kings (that idea probably arose from thinking about
Isaiah 60.3: 'kings to the brightness of your dawn'), and if
you look closely Matthew does not even tell us that there
were three of them, though the threefold nature of their
gifts is certainly suggestive of this possibility.

What we can be sure about is that they were Gentiles, coming from outside the covenant people of Israel. The Feast of
the Epiphany is the celebration of the Manifestation of
Christ to the Gentiles. The magi's eventual arrival at
Bethlehem signified that the coming of God's kingdom that
began with the birth of Jesus was a divine act that held significance for all people, whatever their race or wherever they
came from. Most of those who will read these words of mine
are likely to be Gentiles, just as I am, and we should be grateful that the magi were there to worship the Christ child as
representatives on our behalf.

The followers of Jesus during his lifetime were Jewish and,
though he healed those Gentiles in need who crossed his
path (the Roman centurion's servant, Matthew 8.5–13; the

Syrophoenician woman, Mark 7.24–30), he knew that his immediate ministry was to the people whom God had been preparing over the centuries: 'I was only sent to the lost sheep of the house of Israel' (Matthew 15.24). After the resurrection, the Church came slowly to realize that what had been a practical necessity during Jesus' earthly life, was no longer a limitation on the scope of the gospel in the age of the Spirit. When the believers in Jerusalem heard of how God had been at work in the life of the centurian Cornelius, they exclaimed, 'Then God has given even to the Gentiles the repentance that leads to life' (Acts 11.18). If they had remembered the magi, they might not have seemed quite so surprised. All the social, cultural and religious differences that had appeared so significant in the past, were abolished with the coming of new life in Christ, for 'There is no longer Jew or Greek, there is no longer slave or free, there is no longer male or female; for all of you are one in Christ Jesus' (Galatians 3.28).

The magi were also intellectuals, students of the stars and seekers after truth. It took the learned sages somewhat longer than the unlearned shepherds to find their way to Bethlehem, but they got there in the end. Christian faith is not a matter of theological cleverness, but the Church has always rightfully had a place in its ranks for those whose vocation is the scrupulous search for truth.

Prayer

Almighty and everlasting God, who hast made known the incarnation of thy Son by the bright shining of a star, which when the wise men beheld they adored thy majesty and presented costly gifts: Grant that the star of thy righteousness may always shine in our hearts and that for our treasure we may give to thy service ourselves and all that we have; through the same Jesus Christ our Lord.

(Gelasian Sacramentary, eighth century)

Baptism of Christ: All assumed

*Then Jesus came from Galilee to John at the Jordan, to be baptized
by him. John would have prevented him, saying, 'I need to be baptized by you, and do you come to me?' But Jesus answered him,
'Let it be so now; for it is proper for us in this way to fulfil all
righteousness.' Then he consented.*

(Matthew 3.13–15)

All four Gospels, in their different ways, tell us about Jesus'
baptism. In the report of the proclamation of the heavenly
voice, 'This is my Son, the Beloved, in whom I am well
pleased' (Matthew 3.17), we are given insight into the call
that inaugurated Jesus' public ministry. The baptism is a very
important episode in the gospel story. It was also, perhaps
especially for the early Church, a puzzling episode. The
problem is this: John's baptism was a baptism of repentance.
Those whom he plunged beneath the waters of the Jordan
were seeking, in this symbolic way, to gain the washing away
of their past sins. It was the belief of the earliest Christians,
and it has been the faith of the Church ever since, that Jesus
led a sinless life. He, alone of all people, seemed to be the
one for whom John's baptism would be quite inappropriate.
In the account in Matthew, we see the Baptist himself aware
of the incongruity. 'I need to be baptized by you, and do you
come to me?' Jesus' somewhat enigmatic reply is, 'it is proper
for us in this way to fulfil all righteousness'.

What exactly is going on? Although Jesus' close alignment
with the will of his heavenly Father protected him from sin-
ning, his solidarity with humanity did not at all protect him
from temptation. The salvific effect of Jesus' life and death
and resurrection derives from the power and presence of
God that was in him, but its relevance for us derives from the
fact of the full humanity that he shares with us. 'Therefore
he had to become like his brothers and sisters in every
respect, so that he might be a merciful and faithful high
priest in the service of God, to make a sacrifice of atonement
for the sins of the people' (Hebrews 2.17). An early

Christian thinker, Gregory Nazianzus, put it very well when he said that all had to be assumed so that all could be redeemed. Jesus' faithful obedience never fails, so that he does not fall into sin, but nevertheless he is subjected to all the trials that are the common human lot. His baptism is the symbol of this solidarity with us, not in sin but in the contradictions of life in this fallen world. This total assumption of the human condition is most movingly and profoundly expressed in the darkness of Calvary. The one who is both human and divine cries out, 'My God, my God, why have you forsaken me?' (Mark 15.34; Matthew 27.46). In the paradox of the cross, the God-man assumes the experience of God-forsakenness, in order to deliver humankind from its alienation from God.

Prayer

Thanks be to thee, my Lord Jesus Christ, for all the benefits thou hast won for me, for all the pains and insults thou hast borne for me. O most merciful Redeemer, friend and brother, may I know thee more clearly, love thee more dearly, and follow thee more nearly, day by day.

(St Richard of Chichester)

Postscript

Does the universe make sense?

All human beings are going to die, and eventually the universe itself is going to die, either through collapse or through decay. Such widespread mortality raises the question of whether a universe that eventually ends in apparent futility actually makes sense. Is it really a creation or is it, in fact, a chaos, without any final meaning to it? A Nobel prize-winning physicist, Steven Weinberg, writing from an atheist perspective, once said that the more he understood the universe the more it seemed pointless to him. This question of whether the world really makes sense was with us, in one form or another, throughout Advent.

Our conclusion has been that the universe does make sense and it looks like something adding up to what could convincingly be called a creation, but this is only because there is a theological story of things to come that complements the scientific story of the way things are at present. In addition to the tale of the 'old creation', there is the further tale to tell of God's 'new creation'. It has been central to the argument that two conditions must be satisfied if that extended story really is to hang together as an account of true and everlasting fulfilment.

The first condition is that the new creation has to come out of the old creation as its redeemed transformation. Otherwise there would be no ultimate point in this present world existing. If in the end it is to be thrown away, and ourselves with it, why bother with it or us in the first place? The people who live the resurrected life of the new creation have to be the same people who lived and died in the old creation, so that they are not discarded when their lives here come to an end. We have called this condition, continuity.

The second condition is that the new creation has to be radically different in its character from the present creation. The world to come has to be a place where death and suffering are no more. It would not make sense just to play out a repeat round of this present kind of history. We have called this condition, discontinuity.

Our best clue to how these twin conditions of continuity/discontinuity might be satisfied is given us by the event that is our main source of insight into God's ultimate purpose for creation, the resurrection of Jesus Christ. It is Jesus himself who lives again and whose body still bears the scars of his passion. Here is continuity. Yet he is not just revived for another spell of earthly life, for he is alive for evermore, risen and glorified, and his body can appear and disappear in locked rooms. Here is discontinuity.

The resurrection of Jesus on the third day is the great seed event from which the new creation has already begun to grow. The worlds of the old and new creations exist, in some sense, 'side by side' today, so that reality has the inbetween character of a mixture of 'already and not yet'. However, eventually the whole of the old will be transformed into the new. This redemptive unfolding of the new creation is a great act of divine power and love, bringing about the completion of God's purposes. The fundamental fact that makes sense of the universe lies beyond itself in the steadfast love of its creator, who will never allow anything of good to be lost and who works unceasingly for the completion of the divine redemptive purpose. Just as Advent and Epiphany lead on in the Church's year to Good Friday and Easter, so it is the coming of the new creation that makes fully intelligible God's purpose in bringing the present world into being.

Questions

The purpose of this book has been to try to help its readers think about some of the deep insights of the Christian faith.

I have not written it as someone who thinks he knows all the answers, but as someone who is a fellow-traveller on the road of Christian exploration. We are all sometimes in the position of needing to respond to a comment or question about our faith that is made in our presence, and so it is helpful to be prepared to make adequate use of these opportunities for witness. If as an individual or in a group you have used this book as study material, you may want to think how it would help you to respond if someone made a remark like one of these that follow. For convenience they are grouped in a way approximating to the sections of the book, but I hope that you will be able to make use of the whole experience of our Advent and Epiphany meditations in responding to them.

Why bother about Advent? Let's get on with Christmas.
Hope is just whistling in the dark to keep your spirits up.

'Christ will come again'. What on earth does that mean?
When you're dead, you're dead. That's that.
Can't believe all that stuff about Adam and Eve and the apple.
Shall I see my husband/wife again?

Seeing's believing, isn't it?
Why should I worry? God will forgive me – that's what he's like.
Religious people just keep going on about sin. What a gloomy lot!

What's the soul then – sort of ghost? Can't believe in that.
I don't want to live for ever – dead boring.
Heaven? That's just pie-in-the-sky.
I don't want to go to heaven if my dog won't be there.

The Church uses Mary to keep women subservient.
No one believes in hell today.
Doesn't matter what you believe – no one really knows what's true.

Christmas is for kids (and a booze-up).

What's God really like? How can we be sure?

How could God let all those little children in Bethlehem get killed?

It's all right for him up in heaven – what about life in this hell on earth?

Jesus was a good man, all right, but what's so special about that?

What can I hope for?

The struggle between good and evil will just go on for ever – no side can win.

The universe is pointless.